W9-CFF-132

Palm Springs

Palm Springs

The Landscape
The History
The Lore

MARY JO CHURCHWELL

Ironwood Editions

ISBN 0-9713016-0-3

Library of Congress Catalog Card Number: 2001118347

*For Mary Paradise Stephens, my mother,
my dining companion, my confidant,
my mentor, my best friend*

Contents

Author's Note

Although I have maintained an earnest effort to achieve factual accuracy, the storyteller who lives in my head has somewhat had her way with what is told in these pages. Nevertheless, except in one case where someone needed anonymity, all the names in this book are of real people. All the places exist. All the events are based on fact. And even though I have not let out any secrets, at the same time I know it can be jarring to find a piece of your family history in someone else's book. I apologize for that.

ONE

O Prickly Pear Pioneers!

There are some desert turtles or horned toads or chuckawallas in Palm Springs or vicinity that should be entered in the Plaza Fiesta tomorrow. Although the turtles hibernate during the winter, when placed on the warm pavement and allowed to sun themselves there for a few hours they soon become active and are ready for a turtle race. The same applies to horned toads and chuckawallas.

—THE DESERT SUN 1938

*O*NE OF US exiting I-10 at Palm Springs was clearly not commuting to work. You could tell by the mountain bike tethered to the bumper, by the baggage strapped to the rack on the roof—and all kinds of things stacked on the floor and passenger seats, too many things by the way the old van was riding. There had been no good-byes, no one to see me off with solemn embraces. We had given the marriage a final try, Stew and I, strangers together in that little cabin. For years I had been on my way home to Palm Springs, to the warm web of family. Now I was here.

If you are moving from the mountains of Idaho to the dead-level desert of the Coachella Valley, as I was doing this hot day in September, you won't be impressed by the land-scape. You have to wonder was there ever so much wasteland in all the world. People call it barren when they fly over it, and describe it later on the golf course as *nothing*. "There's nothing out there." And yet, as negative as the scene appeared, the sandy nothingness stirred me to my roots. Every mile was a pleasure, a crawl back through my past.

Directions had been given over the phone. I turned left and stopped at an electric gate behind which my widowed mother lived alone (but in cozy proximity to her fine, adorable great-grandchildren), in a tract of development called—absurdly, at least to me—Sunshine Villas. I scanned the directory and punched in three numbers. "Hi. I'm here," I said to the microphone. "But not permanently," I meant to add. To move in with your mother when you are well into middle-age is to fall from grace somehow.

With a creak, the gate opened onto a tarmac that split into three private roadways, the names, simplicity itself: Sunshine Way, Sunshine Drive, Sunshine Circle. Midway into the second block, I arrived, refugee-like, at my mother's villa. She did not rush from her La-Z-Boy to welcome me. This was like old times for her, taking in lost relatives. Most likely she was thinking through the changes I would bring, the new noises and smells in her air, the intrusion into her privacy. As for me, I had a sudden, sure sense that this was an important moment, a beginning or an end of something, and I was scared to find out which. So I just sat there, not wanting to turn off the engine, as if it might never start again. But I did turn the key, and the strange business of living at Sunshine Villas began.

* * *

The nature of a desert is to be one thing in September and quite another in March, when mockingbirds sing at every turn and wildflowers bloom in all the vacant lots, the sand verbena sprouting in a startling way, the pink-lavender blossoms climbing all over each other. Inspired by the new season, and feeling in need of exercise, I tuned up the mountain bike. Though a clunker by my son's standards, it took me, in the days to come, on long solos across town. On and on I rode, until I had visited all my old neighborhoods, every corner, half a dozen times. "You won't like what you see," my mother had warned. "And what you see you won't recognize." She was wrong on at least some counts.

True enough, the MFK soda fountain was gone, long torn out, and with it the Village Theater, where a few coins on a Saturday afternoon once filled a kid's every need. But some of the old buildings were still here in exactly the same spots, the same restaurants and bars and T-shirt shops. The Plaza Theater stood unchanged: the rich red carpet and velvet ropes, the ceiling that held half a sky in its starry curve. Also unchanged, from an even earlier time, was the old Catholic church where my grandmother Paradise fingered rosary beads in an atmosphere of incense and candles. And there, further on, the little house with the red shutters where my sisters and I were excellently raised in a golden haze of sleep and play. A little imagination can restore the cramped back bedrooms and the tiny kitchen, wherein my definitive Midwestern mother, to her everlasting credit, kept the cookie sheets hot and on the move.

I write all this neither in a spirit of self-revelation nor as an exercise in total recall, but to explain why I added the public library to my rounds, for it was here that I could further indulge in my nostalgia and in the process fill the gaps in my knowledge of Palm Springs, in a history that is to a great extent my own history. The ride over was short. Out the gates of

Sunshine Villas, across Sunrise Park, up the walkway, and in five minutes flat I was inside the building. Here I found a light, airy space filled with people perusing newspapers, magazines, and books. I recognized a few as kindred souls. Were they reading about Palm Springs? Probably not. Our shelf of local lore is woefully short. And except for several handsome photo studies, it is disappointing in both quality and scope. Least admirable are the books, both fiction and non-fiction, that present a city of sheer, sun-drenched hedonism, a *swanky desert playground*, a *gold-plated mirage*, a *ring-a-ding resort*—to choose actual words from three sources within arm's reach. Whether such rhetoric is pervasive enough to taint the city's reputation I can't say. But certainly it does not help us to understand, in richly sympathetic ways, the city's true character.

I give you by way of illustration Norman Mailer's *The Deer Park*, a novel that spends 375 pages calling Palm Springs *Desert D'Or*, "a town," in Mailer's words, "built out of no other obvious motive than commercial profit." How could such a distinguished writer, two-time winner of the Pulitzer Prize, produce such a dreary story? asked one reviewer for the *New York Times*. My guess: Mailer thought it up; he actually spent less than an hour in Palm Springs.

The place looked no better seen through the eyes of reporter Ray Mungo. "Unique and morally bankrupt" is how he describes it in *Palm Springs Babylon*, a city "made up of hotels, nightclubs, bars, resorts, famous parties, cheats, real estate scams, bankruptcies, organized crime." Mungo's history is Elvis Presley hosting unbridled parties at his Las Palmas estate, Frank Sinatra being helped off his knees "after collapsing, drunk, at Ruby's Dunes," former president Gerald Ford "rummaging through the tomatoes and avocados" at Ralph's Mar-

ket "just like any other retiree in shorts," and Liberace intro-
ducing new levels of decadence to the "old whore of a town"
that had seen everything, or thought it had.

Cleveland Amory, best-selling author and animal lover ex-
traordinaire, is no less condescending. While on assignment for
Harper's, he took the occasion to deliver another slap. It is
Amory who tells us that the history of Palm Springs is beneath mention—"lost in antiquity," as he phrases it, and "none
too precious." Which is all of Amory that I'm inclined to
quote.

While Mailer, Mungo, and Amory suggest a world that may
or may not have existed, such rhetoric can shape attitudes.
And while I have as much trouble as the next person with il-
lusions and reality, they threw my very childhood into question. Wondering what else might be skulking on those shelves,
I wandered the aisle until there was nothing left to learn there.
At which point, I dropped the various threads of my life and
pursued full time my sentimental education. In the reference
room of the library, I ransacked the stacks of vintage *Villager*
magazines. I scrolled through reels of microfilm, the pages of
the *Desert Sun* unreeling effortlessly decade after decade. Now
I was truly on to something. Poking around still further, I
found a glass-fronted bookcase, its locked door suggesting a
treasury of knowledge that was merely worshipped, never
consulted (hence the librarian's amazement when I asked for
the key). Here in their dull colors of moss and somber brown
were dozens of limited editions, their titles in faded gold, their
bindings slack from a thousand readings. The specter of those
who wrote the books haunted me. I imagined such an author
glancing up from his rolltop desk, laying aside his pen to light
a pipe, weary, but satisfied with the day's work.

Spreading my four selections on the long worktable before me, I settled in for another very long afternoon. Dipping into the pages of *The Southern Sierras of California*, I saw Charles Frances Saunders on the "wind-beaten summit of San Jacinto," and again on "yonder heaving ridges of sand," with their "gay conventions" of wildflowers. Turning to *Wonders of the Colorado Desert*, I came across George Wharton James at the hot mineral spring, where the occasional tourist took the cure:

> Immediately the bather reaches this quicksand he sinks with a swift motion that makes the heart leap unless he is prepared. In a moment the warm liquid sand closes around the body and it feels as if he were being sucked in and down by the clinging tentacles of some living creature that had the power to hold the body in a most soothing and satisfactory embrace. Then, suddenly, with a convulsive effort, but as gentle as if one were being lifted up in his mother's arms, the water of the shaft gives an upward "bubble" upon which the bather is lifted completely out and the pool becomes placid. If one has not been warned of the peculiarity of this spring, however, he is pretty sure to feel genuine terror until he has personal experience of its safety.

In *Stories and Legends of the Palm Springs Indians*, I found Francisco Patencio under the ancient sycamores of Chino Canyon, his oral accounts, what had been passed on from one generation to the next, reduced to a slim paperback, a woefully scant record of a vanished way of life:

> We used the leaves of the palm trees to thatch our roofs and sides of our houses . . . The floors of the houses were

covered with soft skins and fine woven blankets. At night, before it was time for the children to go to bed, some mother would tell a story. Then children from other houses would come to listen. They would lie around on the rugs and skins, and some would go to sleep before the story was started . . . They would make many books, all stories that Indian mothers told their children . . . They would tell them stories about the sun and the moon and the stars, the air, the wind, the water, the sky, the world, and the people, and the animals and fish upon it.

I found it hard to put down Patencio and harder still to put down J. Smeaton Chase. Chase was special. He was a romantic spirit who did for our desert what landscape painters did for the sea. With literary style, he raised and set the sun, sensed the message in a vacant tortoise shell, saluted the desert mice who "chummed up" with him by many a campfire, where they equally amused and amazed him "by taking headers into the hot ashes at every opportunity, as though the thought of being baked alive was irresistible." Whether it was in Palm Canyon, seized by the motion picture people "for their antics"; or on the sand dunes "worked up" by the wind into "domes, half domes, waves, crevasses, all the shapes that snowdrifts take"; or on the shores of the Salton Sea, where a few dead trees were all that "broke the melancholy expanse" and the decayed bodies of fish "added no charm to the landscape or the breeze," like Kilroy, he had been there.

It was in the reference room that I met our city librarian, Margaret Roades. There being only so much we can learn from books, in the mid 1980s she set out with video camera, microphone, and several patient interviewers to record the memories of the Palm Springs pioneers, my old teachers and parents' friends among them. "Prickly Pears" they were styled, suggesting a comparison to the local cacti, lovely in full bloom, and barbed. Since the interviews, so many of these elders, having endured into their eight and ninth decades, have passed on to become only rambling stories in the minds of others.

With pleasure I viewed the Prickly Pear tapes, not just once, but twice. Palm Springs was quite the village back then. *Village.* That's what they called it. I like the word, with its suggestion of neighborly laughter, borrowed cups of sugar, and gossip over the laundry-lines; of women in sundresses tending geraniums on the windowsills and raising lettuce in the chicken yards out back; of Main Street merchants in starched white aprons stirring up little eddies of dust with their brooms, and whistling, whether or not they had something to whistle about. Well, maybe it wasn't exactly that way, but it was something like it.

Having given over their morning to recording the past, the Prickly Pear pioneers tell us about their everyday rounds of work and play, a spouse shuffling in and out of the living room occasionally called upon to do some of the remembering. They speak with deep breaths and sighs, fretting over every word they choose, slapping their forehead when confused for a name. Slowly it comes back to them. *Just the other day* was nineteen and thirty-eight, the year of the flood.

The Whitewater River was all over the place. It was everywhere. It ravaged the whole valley all the way to the Salton Sea . . . everywhere.

We never left the house for two days. The water was coming right down Indian Avenue. The water was com-

8

ing down Baristo. Half of that Builders Supply wound up in Coachella. Man, I mean it just went right down the wash. I mean, you could see a lot of real estate changing hands. It came through Frances Stevens School. There's three or four cars buried out there in the playground. I mean, it just undercut them and buried them. They just stayed there, that was all.

Yesterday . . . that was the earthquake of forty-eight.

I remember looking up and seeing the dust from rocks sliding down the mountain. The dust cloud from the hills at Desert Hot Springs, on the fault, was just like an atomic mushroom. The rocks rolled down through the Tennis Club, and every plate glass window in town was broken. We had the whole neighborhood gang in the middle of the street and got the little old lady across the road, too. She was stuck in the house with the door jammed. It went on and on and on, and the aftershocks, too—I don't think they scaled it. There are no numbers.

Occasionally shifting their gentle old bones to get comfortable, they let their thoughts wander over things remembered and still deeply felt, little individual tales in some way connected. The memory of living without electricity or running water, of cooking over a potbelly stove, of reading by kerosene lamp still thrills them. It was a good life, a heroic life.

We had an iceman. He came once a week. He came from Banning in a little truck with burlap over the chunks of ice. By the time he drove to Palm Springs over that washboard road, and the heat . . . and went around and delivered these chunks of ice—we'd put them in a little icebox—by the end of the day there wasn't any ice. So if you wanted to have company at all, you better have them that day by noon, so you'd have some ice.

The problem was not getting answers, but thinking up questions. What did they do for recreation, if, in fact, they thought they needed recreation?

There were monthly dances at the Frances Stevens School. And Earle Strebe would show movies there every Saturday night in the auditorium. But otherwise there were just parties and picnics, a lot of picnics and moonlight rides . . . they'd bring their own horses.

There was a band of fifty or so horses just roaming around trying to find something to eat. The Indians caught a few of them themselves, and they actually belonged to them, but there were so many that were born that they just didn't want them. So they just roamed around. My sister started a stable here by catching Indian ponies and breaking them and renting them.

In the summertime we were down to practically nothing . . . maybe 50 or 60 people, something like that. There were 58 Indians, I think. For pastime sometimes we'd get out and sit on the curb there across from the Desert Inn on Palm Canyon and take a .410 shotgun and shoot bats. Out of the air. The constable would be with us. He'd shoot them too, you know.

If you supposed you were going to die within the decade you might think of a few more things worth mentioning. Like the fire in Palm Canyon.

Boy, you could see that for hundreds of miles, that smoke going up there. It was really something. And there was no putting it out, because it was so hot you couldn't get near it. And it went through so fast—a palm tree with those skirts down was just like a chimney you know. That draft goes up and boy, it just sends the sparks. They sent the CCC boys out and a lot of portable generators and these wire brushes and tried to clean them up, but that all goes away. There's hardly any trees around that hasn't been burned sometime or other. They're hardy and they survive. Yeah, they always come back.

They progress from one topic to another, holding up pictures, calling off names, describing how it was.

This is the El Mirador Hotel, taken in 1936, before they ever built the prisoner of war barracks there and the Tourney Hospital. That is Dr. [Albert] Einstein and Mrs. Einstein at the El Mirador Hotel. And this was the city dump. It caught fire and burned for about twenty years. This is an early picture of Frank Sinatra. Sinatra was a spoiled brat. We had slot machines down here like crazy. Every hotel office—or just about—had a slot machine in it. Every restaurant had a slot machine. Drugstores had the slot machines, liquor stores. They were all taken out and replaced by jukeboxes.

Out of their mouths tumbles, oh, just about everything.

Rattlesnakes were our chief hobby. At one time we had eighteen rattlers in a cage on the porch. And we always counted them when we came home at night, because we slept on the porch. And one night we had seventeen—we missed one. And we hunted everywhere . . . we couldn't find it. And so we went to bed out there, and the next morning we released a king snake and in five minutes it found that rattler, and I got a movie—full movie of him—when he finally struck the rattler headfirst and swallowed him. And I pinched off the rattles, just before he went down.

They were young, these pioneers, and so was their village. Everything was just outside the front door. The world was no bigger than that. The good old days. The way it used to be. You could sing it in chorus with them.

*   *   *

Forgive me, but before arriving at my mother's doorstep I had generally shunned local history, so preoccupied was I by family affairs. Well now I was fairly wallowing in it, happily living ninety percent of my life in the past, my brain fairly humming with half-told stories. Now it came home to me that I could write a book that would contribute to the understanding of my native city, perhaps change its image as artificial, insubstantial, and perverse, its history "none too precious." I could submit evidence of a creative past, a past worthy of respect, with plenty of space reserved for Mother Nellie Coffman, Auntie Pearl McManus, Judge John Guthrie McCallum, Dr. Welwood Murray, and Zaddie Bunker, the Flying Grandmother. These were the people who mattered so much that there is little chance of understanding Palm Springs without taking them into account. Here was a cast of characters that Mungo had dismissed and Mailer had never imagined.

So that was the beginning, and I have no idea where it will

end. In the meantime, having cast myself in the role of writer, I gladly play the part. In the many houses and apartments my long life has occupied, never have I had a room to myself (and because my dear children have ruled my life, never more than five minutes' peace unbroken). Now I have a room, without asking, a personal retreat with a door that locks and a view of an outer, sunlit world massively dominated by mountains. I have a bookshelf and a growing reference library. I have a good light over my bed to read by, and enough large cross-stitched pillows (my mother's contribution) to prop myself like a sultan. I have a worktable, a telephone, and a desk pushed against a windowless wall, which puts the view behind me. I have a computer and a thickly-padded chair of the sort designed for long hours at the keyboard (the sound of tapping gives my bedroom a secret life unlike that of any other bedroom in Sunshine Villas). This chair, admired by everyone, has a complement of adjustable positions that allows me to lean forward (to type) or recline backward (to think). I can tilt, swivel, and roll from my desk to my worktable—a vivacious sprawl of photocopies, clipped columns from the *Desert Sun*, overdue library books, drifts of notepaper, a dozen or so doodlepads and dull pencils—this disorder bothers me but I hope to pull out of it a clean narrative. All of which leaves few guesses as to how I spend my days. When an invitation comes my way I hesitate. Well, I'm busy working on my book, I say, using a formula that has grown increasingly weary. It takes all my time now. Truth is, I've gotten snobbish about how long the people I'm with have lived in Palm Springs. And even then, I'm only interested if they say things like, "Want to hear something weird?" That's catnip to me.

"So what's this book about?" someone will ask.

"Oh, you know," I laugh and say, "it's about Palm Springs, the good, the bad, the completely ridiculous." I confess that my reply sounds hollow. But it's unlucky to speak of your work-in-progress.

TWO

Shaping a Resort

It was a rough night in the Cadillac division of the Racquet Club Saturday when young Jerry Norman Evans, 16, lost control of his car on Indian Avenue and clipped six fin tails in succession. When the orchestra leader stopped the music to announce that six Cads were involved in a wreck in the parking lot, practically every male in the room jumped up to find out if one of the six was his.

—THE DESERT SUN 1950

*T*HE SIGN ON the fence says you can get thirty-two people in this pool at one time. Today I have it to myself, a blessing, no grandkids flippering around in their plastic swans, no small talk required, no questions from the neighbors, well-meaning people for whom questions are the best means of getting acquainted. "You're—*who?*"

I am the woman staked out under the big umbrella, the one you don't want to disturb (but should you show the slightest interest in local history, I would seize your wrist and deliver an hour-long lecture). I'm not technically "on vacation," but I could be mistaken for someone who is. Like any visitor, I know what I'm here for. The postcards, the T-shirts, the travel brochures are true: Paradise exists.

"Aren't we lucky! Don't we live in a wonderful place!" My

mother says that, seems like, ten times a day. Although she never speaks specifically of the reasons, what she means is our magical landscape of flowers and lawn, our winters of no snow, God be praised. The last time it snowed in Palm Springs was over twenty years ago, a fragile few inches of powder that remained on the ground only long enough to astonish children and make them wonder what it was.

Trees absolutely dominate—wonderfully—the landscape beyond the pool. Since everything will grow in Palm Springs, everything is planted, which makes newcomers from the rural Midwest feel right at home. *Trees.* Here in the desert, where almost no trees grow on their own accord. In fact, Sunshine Villas has ransacked the ends of the earth for these trees. The Aleppo pine, native to Syria, is a case in point. I assume these are Aleppo pines because one died last spring during an Aleppo pine epidemic and the gardeners had to cut it down. I can identify with certainty only four or five trees around here and the Aleppo pine is not one of them.

On the other hand, I'm dead sure those are evergreen pears, nicely arranged and blooming with wonderful effect. *Sunset Magazine* tells us they come from Asia, are easy to grow, tolerant of many soils, and "a great success in climate zones where temperatures remain above freezing." Credit Africa for our sumacs ("can be messy on pavement"), Brazil for our jacarandas ("needs regular but not frequent irrigation"), China for our camphors ("drops leaves quite heavily"), and the Eastern Mediterranean for our carobs ("roots will break sidewalks"), wherein our English sparrows noisily nest. Given enough water, such a landscape of trees can crop up anywhere. A network of buried pipes creates a rainbelt head high that travels so predictably it's possible to walk through the heart of it and remain dry, given proper attention to timing.

The stock for our eucalyptus ("dramatic skyline tree . . . a Japanese print in its mature silhouette") came from Australia in the 1880s, during a crusade to forest the gaunt treelessness of Southern California, as if Southern California were a kind of failed forest that needed only the hand of man to restore. Eucalyptus was selected for its quick growth, and for the notion that its aromatic odor somehow accelerated the healing effect of the climate (it was also supposed to rid the neighborhood of fleas). Indeed eucalyptus grew well in Southern California, shot up at a rate, some enthusiasts swore, of a foot or more a month. As it turns out, planting eucalyptus on the well-watered lawns of Sunshine Villas was perhaps a mistake. One old monarch has achieved redwood specifications, but so precariously is it balanced on its earthless roots, I'm tempted to make it a point of being present at the exact moment of its collapse.

The best you can say for eucalyptus is that it's not tamarisk, a thoroughly successful tree introduced from Arabia in 1909, that is, before anyone realized that such introductions had their downsides. All tamarisk requires to establish a good stand is a good water supply, and that it has found in our Indian canyons. Slowly and harmfully it spreads along the creek bottoms, elbowing its way past the natives, going as far as the creeks go, and a bit beyond, at the slightest hint of moisture. Today's efforts to control it only speed up the invasion. It both seems and *is* impossible to eradicate. It can only be *managed*, that is, pulled up, dug up, burned, sprayed, bulldozed . . . and still it sends up shoots with a new and vengeful vigor, all over the place, every day of the week.

Since the community of Sunshine Villas is now a large part

of my life, I will venture it further into these pages. To begin with, I shall record that the homes here are a great value as any number of realtors will tell you—cheap by Palm Springs standards. Our three-bdrm units go for around 100 K. That's 1,400 sq ft. in the wind-free south end of town. Two bths, fplc, carpets, cntrl heat and air, cable hookup, attched gar. Four heated pools, as advertised, four Jacuzzis, four lighted tennis courts. Close to shopping and schools. At the close of escrow you will receive a key, a remote, and a three-inch coded card that will open the front gate. You will be issued a number for the intercom system and thus be protected from solicitors, malicious teenagers, and strangers, dangerous and not (the guardhouse for our checkpoint charlie is unmanned for now but is definitely designed to be manned if trouble breaks out). Other keys will give you access to the Mesquite Golf Course next door, where a fantasy of plumbing nurtures another imported forest in the making. Even more remarkable are the ponds that provide habitat to a bewildering variety of waterfowl: egrets, herons, coots (all over the place), American widgeons (as far as the eye can see), wood ducks, cinnamon teals, funny little ruddy ducks, green-winged teals, northern shovelers, pied-billed grebes, Canada geese, ring-necked ducks . . . I've got my bird book, I've got my list . . . somewhere. In the evening, when the golfers, the grounds crew, and the security guards have gone home, trespass is easy.

If, on the grounds of good faith, I may be permitted an aside, it would be to fill in the spaces between the realtor's words with a few details of my own. Sunshine Villas is your basic Palm Springs condominium, a walled community founded on sunshine and sand, complete with its own master plan, homeowner association, board of directors, and pesky set of rules and restrictions designed to maintain order and undermine imagination. What you have is a neighborhood without charm, without character. There are no indications that children live here, no tricycles in the driveways, no basketball hoops bracketed to the garages. "No Pets" says the lawn. As for the villas themselves, they are all of identical structure, so anonymous and plain as to seem ownerless: same picture windows, same chimneys, same patios trimmed off with border beds of flowers and shrubs, identical arrangements over and over, the orange and crimson of bougainvillea too bright for the desert, the petunias too gaudy in their purples and pinks—and positively ghastly when planted side by side. This same conformity prevails clear to the mailboxes, all done in black, possibly because the paint was on sale at the lumber yard.

If I have exposed conditions that are not frequently discussed, I am certain they are ones that secretly engage the minds of many members of our community. At the same time, by the evidence of our monthly meetings, not many of us want to move away. We speak as if it were a privilege to live here, as if it were an act of grace we found ourselves here. If there are limits to our little paradise, it remains undiminished, untarnished.

* * *

There was a time within memory of the Prickly Pear pioneers when Palm Springs showed little signs of the condo mecca it would become. J. Smeaton Chase, who knew it in the far-off days of the 1920s, pictures it so nicely in *Our Araby*:

> The village itself is a place of two or three score of unpretentious cottages scattered along half a dozen palm-

and pepper-shaded streets. We don't run much to lawns and formal gardens: we live in the desert because we like it, hence we don't care to shut ourselves away in little citified enclosures.

Four years after Chase's death in 1923, the *Desert Sun* began publication and thus continued to record the spirit of the place, the small-town world of "Bozo the Clown Returns" and "Stork Delivers Baby Burro to Stables of Bob Bennett" and "Wasp Behavior to be Subject of Lecture"—headlines to gladden the heart. Except that on certain years, in early spring, this traditional mix was put aside for a lead story that had nothing to do with the innocent folkways of folks. "County Cautions Visitors" the headlines would shout with glee at the promise of the follow-up stories that would certainly result. What this item concerned was the unlawful "picking, collecting, removing, mutilating, destroying, and transporting of wildflowers, trees, shrubs, cactus, or other desert plants." Thus armed with a skein of catch-all laws, the wildflower police, in all solemnity, patrolled the countryside, delivering lectures and handing out citations. For tourists who dared to scoff, there was the slammer, where, it was hoped, they would emerge chastened, determined to change their ways. Everyone agreed that tourists could be such a headache. It was also agreed that they were income for merchants, a market for realtors, and work for contractors. They were publicists who penned chirpy letters to loved ones back home in the snowbound East. The wildflowers had to be protected *for* them as much as *from* them. That's how it worked.

Tourists were one thing, armyworms quite another (technically, they were the larvae of the sphinx moth). No sooner had the sand dunes filled with lovingly familiar hues, then here they came, a writhing, pulsating mass of yellow, eating their way across the Coachella Valley. By the time the *Desert Sun* got around to reporting it—"Caterpillars on the March"—the worms had already advanced on the village, all set to strip bare everything in bloom or about to bloom; their progress was tracked with a seriousness usually reserved for armies of men on the march. What happened next is what you would expect to happen, with so much at stake here. Imagine it, all those public-spirited villagers, women and children among them, ransacking their tool sheds for rakes, hoes, and other weaponry of slaughter, striking out in all directions, chopping army-worms to death. It was a gruesome sight, but the wildflowers were saved until they bloomed themselves out.

Those were the days all right. Because there wasn't much bulldozing going on, wildflowers spread to the ends of the earth. All that loveliness, the pink-lavender hues of sand verbena, the bouquets of dune primrose, fragrant as wine, popping into bloom wherever the verbena left them room. Elsewhere and equally lavish were flowers the local nature-minded ladies were delighted to point out: lupines, poppies, dahlias, fuchsias, Canterbury bells, fiddlenecks, five-spots, forget-me-nots—a fraction of these flowers would have been more than enough. You've seen the pictures, the quintessential desert scenes in watercolors and oils, the hummocks of pure white sand, the rocky washes in the fantastic play of sunshine. The flowers in the foreground are done in big bold strokes, the blossoms on the palo verde with light flicks of the brush. Or perhaps it's a smoke tree, its interlacing twigs brimming with the purest aquamarine. Or a desert willow in delicate pink—orchids you think. And in the background, the mountains enshrined in paint—a splash about in the purple wash—with an occasional cloud poised for spatial depth. How many Sunday painters came upon such a scene and at the danger of death by sunstroke refused to put their brushes away until it had been fixed upon their canvass?

* * *

The fall of 1853 was not a good time for wildflowers in the Coachella Valley. If anyone knew how bleak a landscape could be it was Lt. J. G. Parke, the man charged by Washington with finding the most practical railroad route from the Mississippi River to the Pacific Ocean. It was natural that such a wild geology, a land without names, at least without English names, should come slowly to the public eye. A wasteland it was, even for a desert, where this epithet can become seriously overused. Constricted on one side by a rugged mountain range, and on the other by a terra incognita destitute of trees—beyond which there might have been no end of all—Parke had little choice but to push ahead through Palm Springs. Imagine the look he gave his corps companions. How do we describe *this*? A "desert monotony" they decided in their report to Washington, "broken by a clump of palm trees on the north of the trail and a green bank from which springs issue. Nothing is known of the Country."

Years later, to make ready for the actual railroad, Henry Washington and his party surveyed Palm Springs to the base of the mountains, also noting the clump of palm trees and the green bank from which springs issue. For obvious reasons, the route from Los Angeles to Yuma would follow the old stage line: the water supplies along the way were no less important to the steam locomotive than they had been to the horse and mule.

Behind the surveyors came crews of American Indians and Chinese immigrants, teams of men willing to do the monotonous back-breaking work, in all kinds of weather, for long hours and low pay. Milton Sanders Hall won the contract to lay the grade, two feet high to protect the tracks from flooding. He also contracted to deliver the ties—as insecure an assignment as there is in this country, where timber is as rare as rain. For this purpose, he built a road from his mile-high sawmill in Idyllwild to the makeshift town of Hall City, located near today's Cabazon. Halls Grade it was called, this road that wasn't so much a road as a dizzy fourteen-mile-long skidway carved into the precipitous north face of the mountain, by which teamsters hauled wagonloads of felled timber. The work was risky enough to dare the devil, reported Banning historian Tom Hughes. "For besides the regular brakes and roughlocks, they had to tie logs and trees on behind loads to drag in the dirt and thus keep the loads off the rumps of the horses. Yet even then there were accidents. At least two men lost their lives . . . and several teams and wagons were dashed to destruction."

The struggle to complete the line was filled with drama. But this is not something you can know in great detail if you were not there. I find myself wishing that Hall, or someone, had taken the time to write it down. All the same, now that the desert was open for business, the railroad needed settlers to purchase its square-mile sections—the black squares on the checkerboard of desert land. Hence, the nationwide come-hither campaign, the spirit of which survives in the old tale of how ripe oranges were stuck on the branches of Joshua trees and the section then sold as orange groves in production. Mass advertising taught the gullible how to see the desert under the transforming influence of irrigation. Palm Springs, in particular, was illustrated with steel engravings rather than photographs; so artists who had never set eyes on the place were able to exaggerate features like date palms standing in lordly procession, fields of vegetables growing like lush weeds, stone-lined irrigation ditches with water rushing to the top. Perpetual Water Rights . . . best opportunity for Men of Moderate Means . . . Earliest Season in the State . . . Home of the Banana, Date, and Orange. No cyclones, no tornadoes, no blizzards, no frosts, no fogs, no dews, etc. etc. etc. (the very word *earthquake* disappeared from the vocabulary in much the same manner as did the word *flea*). With a fruit-hungry market waiting on the coast, the produce would walk straight out of the orchards, and at a high price, too. Here, in the rain shadow of the San Jacintos, in a self-evident desert ill disposed to the cultivation of crops, the vision couldn't have been happier—or harder to put into practice.

First to climb aboard the Sunset Limited at Los Angeles, in their restless twos and threes, were a mismatched collection of health-seekers, land speculators, and tourists who fancied themselves speculators, who in fact became speculators on sudden impulse. Into such an assemblage the farm families fit perfectly, those uneasy people who had farmed in Ohio or Michigan, then in Kansas or Iowa, and were now for somewhere else. They were coming to a land they knew nothing about; there were no reliable guidebooks, no agricultural manuals, no soil analyses, no weather charts. Surely the conductor looked at them doubtfully when they presented their tickets for Palm Springs, and surely they had to assure him they really meant it. But indeed they must have wondered what they had gotten themselves into as the miles of sandy wilderness rolled by. When the heck were they going to break through to the orange groves?

The train came out of a wide emptiness, tore down the long length of the San Gorgonio Pass, slowed its pace as it approached the Palm Springs station, and finally jolted to a stop, soot and cinders belching from the stack. To step down from the train was to accomplish nothing. Nobody had been expecting a great terminal to rise above the desert, with a marble waiting room and a Victorian clock tower crowned by pigeons. But *this*? This little outpost smothered in piles of glaring white sand? Even more discouraging was the location of the station; it was not smack in the Home of the Banana, Date, and Orange, but two hours distant, at Seven Palms.

It was called Seven Palms for obvious reasons. Back when the desert was still largely unmapped, places were identified for the greenhorn traveler on the basis of how many palm trees were evident: Una Palma, Dos Palmas, Two Bunch Palms, Seven Palms, Twentynine Palms, Thousand Palms—the names meaning water, shade, grass for the horses, and "the relief of verdure for the sorely harassed eyes." For this reason, what we call Palm Springs today was identified as Agua Caliente, the most inevitable name for any place where hot springs bubbled up from the ground.

A variety of conveyances were there to meet the arrivals at Seven Palms—give promoters all the time they need and they will come up with anything. In one little scheme called Palmdale (not to be confused with the present city at the northern edge of Los Angeles County), the efforts of a Boston group extended to laying six miles of narrow-gauge track from the

Seven Palms station to the Palmdale site. The line looked like something a train enthusiast might have built, a hobbyist, and it sure enough was. The rolling stock was three flatcars, two yellow cable cars already old from long service in San Francisco, and a little sawed-off wood-burning engine named the Cabazon, whose history was anybody's guess (to nobody's surprise it had a bad habit of jumping off the track with a suddenness unmatched). Alas for ambition. Palmdale looked good on paper, but without a single act of construction, the project was abandoned for lack of water, and with it, the little toy train.

The engine, flatcars, and tracks were loaded onto the big Southern Pacific for shipment to Bakersfield, thereby stranding the two cable cars in mid-desert—a cheerless yellow ruin that astounded prospectors with its strange insignia Market Street. The redwood railroad ties came to a better end. Having caught the eye of certain enterprising villagers in need of lumber, entire sections of track were torn up to build homes, one of which is on display in the center of the city, lending charm and focus to the Village Green. The fact that the house has been separated from its original foundation, loaded on wheels, and set down amid modern shops and restaurants, and that the house itself accommodates modern air conditioning and electric lights, is of little consequence. This house is the real thing, a total experience inside and out. Not a square inch of wall-to-wall carpet disfigures the squeaky wooden floors. No silky peach-colored wallpaper or floor-to-ceiling mirrors mar the plain white walls. No evergreen room freshener covers up the blended scents of linen, horsehair, and old lace.

First-time visitors to the Little House (as we affectionately call it) enter with a sense of surprise and delight as they take in the cozy domesticity of the four small rooms, where Cornelia White closed out her days. Here is Miss Cornelia's gingerbread kitchen, the wood-burning stove, the pitcher pump, the butter mold, the "sad" iron, the meat grinder, and all sorts of cast iron cookware, everything in sight and ready to use, so unlike modern kitchens where everything is hidden in artfully designed cabinets. Here is Miss Cornelia's dining room, the four brocade-seated chairs waiting for her guests, the polished Duncan Fife table in whose center a vase with painted grape leaves holds a dainty spray of yellow asters, the year's brittle last blooms. Here is her bedroom, the old cherrywood four-poster with flowers and leaves carved into the headboard, the hand-stitched quilt smelling of crushed lavender. Here is her living room, the braided rugs, the lace curtains, the faded settee wearing its doilies like snowflakes, the rolltop desk with the curved front that slides back to reveal useful-looking drawers and pigeonholes, the rocking chair where she read in the evening over a mug of hot chocolate. The curators have cleaned the lamps, snipped the wicks, and set out her Bibles.

On the east wall, framed in wood, is a painted Miss Cornelia, a wren of a woman, fine-boned, fine-skinned, her gray hair pulled back from a central parting to form an untidy bun. Even though the artistry is flat and amateur—simply dabs and splashes of color—it nonetheless captures the headstrong eyes, the determined set of the unrouged lips. So who was Miss Cornelia? The picture I have developed is a collage of images pieced together from the files our local historical society labors to keep in good repair. What I have found is something of a square peg, a woman who found her true identity in fringed jackets, riding britches, and the kind of jungle helmet that the adventurous wear. And indeed, in this era of stylishly dressed women, of high lace collars, floor-dragging petticoats, and preposterous, air-borne hats, Cornelia had an adventurous spirit, a story worth telling.

She was a child on a family farm in western New York State. After successfully defending herself against ten boisterous siblings, eighteen-year-old Cornelia toured Europe for a year, perhaps looking for a place of her own. She became one well-traveled woman. She went to the Pacific Northwest with a mining expedition. She went to the Arctic with her brother. She went to North Dakota and taught home economics, carpentry, and plumbing at the university there. And even that wasn't the end of it. Except that her next adventure, an undertaking of no small proportions, would be neither her best nor her wisest.

Because frankly, 1912 was not a good time to be packing off to Mexico, even though it seemed like all of North Dakota was doing just that. Picking up bag and baggage, Cornelia joined the migration amid the distraction of the Mexican Revolution, that is to say, while Mexico was being ravished by a number of different armies, those of Pancho Villa and Emiliano Zapata contributing more than their fair share.

Upon landing in Sinaloa, Cornelia settled down on a vast tract of wilderness that North Dakota Senator William Lemke had subdivided twenty years earlier. Here, among succeeding waves of revolution, a colony of perhaps two thousand Americans were trying to create a new social, economic, and political destiny for themselves. Invariably there would be a fragile interlude of peace; then the customary violence would begin again, making things impossible. Palm Springs pioneer Carl Lykken, who was also there at Sinoala, gives us a glimpse of what it was like, a few short paragraphs of what could have been a darn good yarn.

Carl and Cornelia had known each other from the beginning. Having met at the University of North Dakota, they renewed their acquaintance in Lemke's colony, a tract that Carl himself had surveyed and mapped. "It was beautiful country," he told an interviewer, meaning Sinaloa. "And you can imagine how anyone from North Dakota would like that climate down there—it was like heaven."

In June 1913 the rebels took Durango, forcing thousands of panicky Americans to flee Mexico for good. Very few remained, Carl and Cornelia among them, huddled in their adobe homes, in a stillness of suspense. Then they, too, decided they had seen enough. "When the revolutionists stole all our horses, our only means of transportation, we knew it was time to get out and stay out."

All told, the little band of refugees numbered six: Carl Lykken, Cornelia White, Cornelia's sister Florilla White, and three other die-hard adventurers. It was eighty miles by handcar to safety, one jump ahead of the devil. And they didn't dawdle for a moment. "They'd burned all the bridges and there were no trains. We had a rough time getting our handcar over some of those places. The ties were all burned away, only the rails were left. We'd give the car a good shove and get over it."

Through the second night they crept, everybody taking turns pumping, convincing themselves that they did, too, know where they were going. The country had become so notorious a place for bandits, men who blandly shot people in the head, that no one in the party was surprised when they were flagged down and searched, their every bundle prodded and poked. And no one could believe their luck when they were sent on their way. Shortly after they reached the American transport ship waiting in Mazatlan—at which point they surely thanked God *that* was over—Sinaloa fell to the revolutionists.

Adios, Old Mexico. Done, but not forgotten. Although the White sisters, both on the verge of confirmed spinsterhood, could endure no more chaos and revolution, frontier life had not lost its appeal. After a hurried exit from San Diego, they migrated to Palm Springs, an obscure little village that Florilla had discovered quite by chance the year before. The place was wonderful, more than wonderful: the shifting light and color of the mountains, the canyons inviting adventure and exploration, the inexhaustible space, the ease and openness of life unconfined in gossipy parlors. If you lived in San Diego or Los Angeles, you had to fit yourself to the demands of your neighbors. You had to play by the rules. Here you were free to arrange the village snug around you, like a blanket. You could lead the good life, that is, your own life. It was no more complicated than that.

If Mexico was Paradise lost, then Palm Springs was Paradise regained. Luckily, the White sisters arrived long after Welwood Murray had decided to retire from the hotel business. For ten thousand dollars, they bought the Palm Springs Hotel. And while they were at it, they invited Carl Lykken, then working in Los Angeles, to share their place in the sun. "I accepted the invitation and never left."

* * *

Miss Cornelia's little house shares the Village Green with the venerable adobe home (venerable by Southern California standards) of John Guthrie McCallum, he who figures so conspicuously in the founding of Palm Springs. Brick by brick the adobe was dismantled by bare hands, moved from its original site in the Tennis Club area, and rebuilt with precision into the modest headquarters of the Palm Springs Historical Society, where, between the hours of ten and four, you are welcome to wander around for nothing more than a small admission charge and your signature in the visitors book. If nothing else, the photograph gallery is well worth a visit, for here hangs the most comprehensive collection of its kind in the county, an incomparable source of insight for historians. As a young village, Palm Springs was eminently picturesque to freelance photographers like J. Smeaton Chase, Gail Thompson, A.B. Trott, W. W. Lockwood, and Edward Curtis. Such was their enthusiasm, they carefully framed each loving scene: the Cahuilla women in head scarves and department store ginghams, busy at their baskets, fully aware they are about to be captured in a meaningful village moment; the lively group of health-seekers at the Palm Springs Hotel, the women in ground-sweeping skirts, whacking croquet balls through the wickets, the men at their bridge game under the palms, their wobbly card table weighed down by beer bottles. The picnics, the campouts, the pony races—unlike today, so much of life took place outdoors, in full view of the photographers.

In particular, I like one old photograph of the Seven Palms station. I look at this picture and both see what is in it and what is not. Evidently no one was much interested in the train that day. There are no friends waiting to greet the passengers, no friends waiting to see them off. There are, in fact, no passengers. There is not a soul in sight, not even the stationmaster. The eye travels rapidly—too rapidly—from the empty station to the empty desert beyond. The scene is unsettling to the viewer in exactly the same way it was unsettling to the arriving farm families.

I began by saying that the arrivals, had there been any on any given day, would have found a variety of conveyances waiting to carry them off to the Home of the Banana, Date, and Orange. Marshall Glenn McKinney, a fount of folklore in his lifetime, remembered in particular Otto Adler's unique service, a scheme involving a "large good-natured brown mule" and a hulking wagon with a crude bench "that could, by crowding, seat six people, but seldom if ever did." Here's how it worked:

> Each day that there were goods or passengers to haul, as determined by a single six-mile long, galvanized iron wire, Otto would start the mule up the road toward the railroad station, then step off the wagon, and go back to work at the hotel. The mule knew the road so well it would follow its course even when it was covered by newly blown sand. The railroad station master would load on the wagon any baggage and passengers, and start the mule back down the road to the hotel. That service was never known to fail, even during the worst of sandstorms.

For all that, the One Mule Stage put a sobering perspective on the journey—two spine-jarring hours across some of the sorriest terrain on the globe. George Wharton James was there to describe it:

> If, combined with the wind, there is the cold of the snow of the mountains one feels nearly perished as he takes his seat in the wagon that is to convey him to Palm Springs.

Seated in the conveyance we start on the drive. The wind blows fiercely. The sand particles are borne along in its clutch, and ere we have gone a mile we are covered from hat to shoes with the tiny particles. Women generally wrap themselves up, covering their heads with a shawl. Men of impulsive and irascible temperaments give vent to objurgations loud and deep, above and below their breaths.

Picture it then, the mule up to its hocks in sand, plodding over the accustomed route, driverless in its traces, the numbness of its misery matched by that of the farm families in their travel-stained Sunday best. I can feel the utter horror of it in my own heart, as those eyes accustomed to the homey touches of lilacs and lawns stared ahead in stunned vacancy at a world without trees, without creeks, without hills, with nothing human for miles, not a farm, not a plowed field, not a fence. You simply could not get your bearings. Or as soon as you did they were gone. Was it this sand dune? or that one? or that one over there? Only the mountains made for confident navigation—although such scale reduced you to your proper status in that unbounded space. It was all you could do to keep in mind the date groves and irrigation ditches pictured on the handbills.

James again:

All feel the discomfort of the sandy winds, and some wish they had not come, when, suddenly, in the space of twenty feet, while there seems to be no change in the conditions, the wind ceases and peace and comfort reign. We have passed into the shelter of one of the protecting spurs [of the San Jacintos] which shuts off the wind of the pass as though by a closed and barred door. Now we may shed overcoats and shawls, for neither wind nor cold will disturb us. This is one secret of the great charm and attractiveness of Palm Springs.

The journey by wagon was good preparation for the actual village, in that, after it, no village, however raw, could disappoint. What the farm families found when they got there was a flyblown cluster of "smelly mud-and-brush hogans" and homespun tents pegged down in the shade of the cottonwoods. The few roads there were, laid down in classic American Rectangle, were a chaos of wandering goats, feral dogs, and barefooted Indian kids on horseback. Actually the roads were rutted paths, but they looked like they wanted to be roads and soon would be.

Ranchers the farmers decided to call themselves, not *farmers*, a word that implied rustic clumsiness and ignorance. Even so, the old mold proved hard to break. Following a brief period of settling in, like farmers, they rolled up their sleeves, spit on their hands, and got down to the work of building dams and digging feeder canals. They planted crop seeds and were delighted to see their fields ripen with alfalfa, asparagus, peas, tomatoes, corn, cucumbers, squash—you name it, that land grew anything. Miraculously, defiantly, the fruits of their labor rolled out of the orchards and into the Southern Pacific's new ice-cooled boxcars, the legend Rush This Through written in big letters on the sides. Fruit was in, nationwide. The urban middle classes, having grown tired of their meat-and-potatoes diet, welcomed all the fresh fruit that the slowly thawing East couldn't provide. It was not an illusion after all. Palm Springs was living up to the promises in the railroad pamphlets. Farming, Wild West style.

That, at any rate, was the idea. But in spite of the ideal combination of irrigated water and maximum sun, the story was over and told within the decade. Even before the ranchers had time to spread themselves out with fences and barns, the flood of 1895 intervened, the Big Flood local history calls it. In a big *whoosh*, the freakishly heavy rain hit the mountainsides and flowed off unchecked—a manic force that swept clear to the Whitewater River, and down the river to the Salton Sink. It was a cruel surprise, this flood in the desert, where water was so precious.

Things seldom end with just one event. With agriculture, there is always something else out there about to make your life miserable. In other words, a flood can work in reverse. No sooner had the ranchers rebuilt their ditches and replanted their crops, men and mules slogging through the mud like farmers, then here it came, another taste of the pitiless and extreme nature of the climate. The Big Drought it was called. This time the rains didn't come when they were supposed to. They didn't come at all, even with the usual prayers. If the romance of ranching had not already fallen apart, it did so in the years that followed. Nothing was spared. The amber waves of alfalfa, the experimental date groves, the vineyards already past the experimental stage, the vegetable fields, the hard-won orchards—everything gone. In effect, the drought killed the Home of the Banana, Date, and Orange. In the desert there's a big difference between seven inches of rain and zero inches of rain, which everyone came to understand very well. In such an atmosphere, there can only be one sequel: you cut your losses and wonder where you might settle next. That a great reservoir of amazingly pure groundwater lay beneath all those deserted, unplanted fields made the Big Drought all the more tragic. Of course, today we have deep wells and electricity and we pump like there's no tomorrow.

* * *

The very weather that ended the agricultural era launched the sanitarium era as physicians, failing to provide relief for disease-ridden America, were forced to subscribe to the climate-cure notion for persistent illness. "Health in the Sunshine" they pitched to the asthmatic, the tubercular, the dropsical, the scrofulous. Again promises outran reality. While some invalids did indeed find health in our desert, many more coughed away what little life they had left, alone and far from home.

Tent therapy the treatment was called, and it was peddled like patent medicine. Doctors, all sharing their instinct for the wrong thing, were advising invalids to avoid contact with the "feared fogs and miasmata," to eat and sleep in the great outdoors, to drink large volumes of highly mineralized water and get plenty of mild exercise, especially horseback riding because the smell of horses was good for the lungs. Nature alone would heal the tubercular formation, rid the system of fever, check the cough, flesh out the wasted body—it was all there, quoted, summarized, and repeated in the medical textbooks and popular press.

As invalids came to the rescue, tent colonies sprang up to receive them. And why not? Cultivating invalids was so much easier than cultivating crops. But no sooner had this new business begun than the myth of health in the sunshine was destroyed by the discovery of a deadly and contagious microorganism impervious to sunny climates. Subtlety was not part of the change in attitude as tuberculophobia took over the Southwest. Consumptives Not Accepted signs went up as health resorts opted to serve as pleasure spots for the healthy. Palm Springs, in particular, became a refuge for wealthy Easterners seeking escape from Eastern winters and the rigidity of Eastern society. At the same time, authors like George Wharton James, darling of the promotional literature scene, continued to lay it on with glowing reports, in effect, keeping the railroad ballyhoo alive and flourishing.

An Englishman by birth, a health-seeker by nature, James gave new life to the phrase "tall, dark, and handsome," *dark* being the operative word. Indeed he was an eyeful: bushy black eyebrows, virile black beard, hair swept back, perfectly tended and utterly black. Physical charms aside, he had a career long and varied. He was a Methodist minister (too handsome for his own good it turned out; he was defrocked under a cloud of scandal). He was a tireless lecturer on all things natural (and therefore good). He was a prolific writer; magazine articles and books flowed from his pen, most notably *Wonders of the Colorado Desert*, the 1907 classic fashioned on the several levels of history, science, and visionary idealism.

James was no armchair writer. He was there, right in the middle of it, sand in his shoes, straining to make each moment yield its image. There is no question that Palm Springs did go to some people's heads.

Upon its northwestern edge I have a camp of my own. Within five and a half hours' ride from my Pasadena home, where library and pictures and piano and flowers and birds and congenial society all conspire to keep me (even were there no loved ones in the home itself), I have found this desert a resting place. Up in a canyon [Chino] on the northeastern slope of the great San Jacinto range, where seeping water makes a "cienega" and gives life to a good size patch of grass; where someone, sometime, planted a fig tree, which has grown to rugged maturity and rich bearing; where there is a hot spring to bathe in, and a cold spring to drink from; sheltered on one side by one of the steepest, if not the steepest and highest wall in the world, and on the other with an outlook over illimitable wastes of desert land, here is where I love to come and rest, think, and write.

Even more enthusiastic than James—if such can be imagined—was fellow countryman J. Smeaton Chase. In the photographer's studio, you'd take Chase for the finest type of Englishman, the name J. Smeaton fitting him on all accounts. One photo in particular shows him wearing a tightly knotted tie, a walrus mustache trimmed to a fussy brush, and a snobby pince-nez on a gold chain looped over his ear. But on a desert trail, the natty, airbrushed image gives way to that of the saddle tramp he was at heart: Chase, stoutly booted against cactus thorns, his face half-hidden under a heavy sombrero that was often "the subject of remark, the comment being that I must suffer from its weight;" Chase, armed with a pistol on one side, a canteen on the other, from which he measured water "in half-hourly gulps."

Chase was a social worker by training and a gifted writer by nature. In an era of long-windedness, he is like a dip in a cool blue swimming pool on a nauseatingly hot day. *California Desert Trails* is particularly revealing. The chapter headings "Poor Man, Poor Land," "Wholesale Suicide of Bees," "Another Thirst-tragedy," "Snakes, Assorted Kinds," and "122 Degrees in the Shade" briefly introduce his rambling four-month-long journey through the Colorado Desert, an overland expedition that begins and ends at his doorstep in Palm Springs. To take in a fair amount of sightseeing, to gain enlightenment through physical suffering, and to record every moment of the entire undertaking, these are the humble goals of J. Smeaton Chase, age fifty-five. If I had done the trip and written it up as cleverly, I would die happy. That's the thing about Chase. He gives you a shining goal to which you might clumsily aspire. He makes you want to set forth into the unknown, notebook clenched firmly in hand.

Obviously unconcerned about comfort, Chase decides his epic journey will begin in the heat of June. But first he must introduce us to his mount, a tough little Indian pony called Kaweah. Then the pack burro Mesquit comes into the story. Almost immediately Chase finds himself in difficulty with the beast. Even so, he is able to describe the fuss and bustle at amiable length:

> Before we were a mile on the way, certain doubts that I had had as to Mesquit's good-will toward the expedition hardened into certainty of trouble. Of all the crimes that are latent in these complicated beasts, the most terrifying is that of lying down under the pack.

Feeling a sudden check on the lead rope, Chase turns around in time to see Mesquit "deliberately gather her feet, kneel down, and compose herself in an attitude of luxury." He dismounts and pulls on the rope.

> She seemed coldly to smile: rope-ended, she put her head to the ground and tried to roll, and though the pack

balked the attempt, I knew by disastrous sounds that ruin was rife among the contents.

Chase prods Mesquit, lightly; she grunts in contempt. He prods her urgently; she kicks. He prods her ruthlessly—"reader, the case was extreme, and the temperature a good hundred and forty in the sun." Mesquit scrambles to her feet and stands quaking, defeated for the time.

Another quarter-mile, and the whole business was en-acted again: a furlong, and yet once more: and, in brief, within the space of six miles . . . eight several battles were fought—I cannot say, *and won*, for the strife was but in-termitted, never closed. And on three occasions the load had all to be thrown off and repacked. This settles it, my fine girl, I said at the second repacking. Kaweah and I can manage without your help.

So saying, Chase takes Mesquit back to Palm Springs, sorts over his baggage—the usual jumble of canteens, barley feed, bedroll, chuck-box, cache of salt, sugar, and tea—cuts it down to the barest needs, and repacks it on Kaweah ("blessing on his tough little carcass"). Then up at dawn and off with the sun, a lighter load and a lighter heart.

Although manifestly not a loner, Chase is alone for most of the journey. Where there is human life, it is made all the sweeter by the harshness of the surroundings. The social worker is revealed in his interest in the Indian villages scat-tered along his route; in the small ranching towns "bare and blinking in the sun"; in the camps of gold miners, "poor wretches who had fallen to the lure"; and in the camps of the Mexican onion-pickers, entire families "loafing and yawning with that air of entire leisure which is a mark of their race, and which I, for one, find rather enviable."

Hot days and hot nights and the end of the journey is still months away. Now all human life, beyond his own, has ceased, and his own is rapidly becoming a nightmare. Everywhere the desert meets him "with a negative." Mirages undulate in alarming fashion, the sun creating lakes of non-existent water, convincing in every detail, except that they retreat before his advance, move ever into the distance. Nothing breaks the vacancy but the skeletons of dead cattle, "sometimes with shreds of hide upon them.

> Leg bones, being easy to manipulate by those ghouls the coyotes, are generally hauled off to a distance, but the skull and ribs with backbone usually stay where the poor brute perished, and coyotes, buzzards, and skunks repair again and again to the feast until the ultimate remnant glistens in the sun, a melancholy monument.

In the meager shadow of his sombrero, he rides on, eyes closed, trusting Kaweah "to pilot us alone." He finds precious little comfort in the canteen, every hot half-hourly gulp throwing him "into immediate perspiration." Constantly his thoughts turn to water, "as Arctic explorers dwell on beef-steaks." Even with rationing, he never knows if he will make the next water hole. What if something goes wrong? What then?

> Those who travel the desert in the middle of summer know well enough that to be two or three hours without water brings a man within the grasp of death. In that terrific temperature one's bodily moisture must be constantly renewed, for moisture is as vital as air. One feels as

if one were in the focus of a burning-glass. The throat parches and seems to be closing. The eye-balls burn as though facing a scorching fire. The tongue and lips grow thick, crack, and blacken. Every organ of the body is deranged, for the drought is not local, but runs through every vein . . . The brain's balance is overthrown and panic adds its terrors to the torment that gnaws each throbbing nerve. Then comes madness, and, whether mercifully soon or cruelly delayed, the end.

Although at times the journey must seem like a monstrous folly, Chase persists, dragging his readers along. We share his amazement when, after 357 fevered pages, he rides into Palm Springs—a moment memorable in more ways than one.

The four months of heat and dryness had left a psychological drought in my bones that I feared might be permanent and drive me into regrettable courses . . . However, the desert itself had the remedy up its sleeve, and produced it . . . when I found myself flooded out of winter camp and subjected to a monumental sousing that brought me within measurable distance of drowning.

I love that: "monumental sousing." J. Smeaton Chase. What else can I say? In endurance and stamina, he was clearly the equal—if not the better—of the Kit Carsons and Jedediah Smiths.

In old age, Chase's love for the still very young village grew even stronger, as the last of his five books reflects. *Our Araby* is, forgive me, unabashedly commercial—Chase in his tedious chamber of commerce phase. Yet the book was immensely popular (and still has its following as the columns of date stamps on my borrowed library copy prove), which indicates that his fervor for the simple charm of village life struck a deep hankering inside America's brutal cities.

Village is a pretty word, though ambitious settlements are keen to disclaim the implied rusticity and to graduate into the rank of town or city. Palm Springs has no such aims, and is well content to remain far down the list in census returns. We decline to take part in the race for Improvements, and are (so we feel, anyway) wise enough to know when we are well off. Rural Free Delivery does not entice us: we prefer the daily gathering at the store at mail-time, Indians and whites together . . . Electric lights? No thanks: somehow nothing seems to us so homelike for the dinner-table as shaded candles, or for fireside reading a good kerosene lamp.

Under the chapter "Amusements," Chase suggests places we must see, attractions we must not, on any account, miss. On and on he goes, long after he should have quit. *Amusement.* What is it? It can be a horseback ride in the canyons, with or without the adjunct of a picnic. It can be a soak in the hot mineral spring. It can be bird study, trout fishing, hunting the local fauna. It can be the Great Spring Wildflower Show, the cacti alone well worth the money ("no one should go through life without interviewing a cholla"). It can be—oh, a hundred and one things that make Palm Springs the best place on earth.

Inasmuch as this was the dawn of California's auto age, had you stuck with *Our Araby* to the very end, you would have picked up "Hints to Motorists." To begin with, you must not venture into the desert stupidly, that is, ill-prepared. You must carry a surplus of water over probable needs. You must carry oil and gasoline over more than probable needs. You must carry a supply of spare tires, tubes, a vulcanizing outfit, a tire gauge, an air pump, a jack. Where there is uncertainty about the route—it is passable, it isn't passable—it is wise to follow the wheel ruts of previous drivers and, Chase might have added, hope they know where they are going and are going where you are going. Of course, the careless could always get into trouble by ignoring the needle on the heat indicator or by wearing the wrong clothes and thereby incurring heat stroke or by stepping on a rattlesnake while shod in open-toed sandals. But those same people could make a mess of crossing Wilshire Boulevard.

By the time *Our Araby* went to press in 1920, cheaper models and the Good Roads Movement had advanced the automobile beyond the sputtering toy of the rich. Everyone was driving the creaky things, moving on tires that exploded with regularity and engines that died almost as often. At the same time, the discovery of important oil fields in the Los Angeles basin gave tourism an enormous boost. In gypsified vehicles, bevies of trippers lit out for the Far West, grub boxes strapped to their bumpers, their trunks stuffed to the breaking point with "everything but their own scenery." Charles Francis Saunders, writing in the era of Chase and James, found the scene bizarre: mattresses carried "debonairly on the roof . . . dogs clinging by their toes to the running-boards . . . cats, parrots, and caged canaries less common but occurring." To sum things up statistically, in one year alone, 1,400,000 people motored a distance of 4,680,000 miles to feed 32 Yosemite bears.

As Palm Springs found its proper place in this vacation landscape, so Charles Francis Saunders, a writer of Pennsylvania Quaker descent, found his proper place in Palm Springs.

Like Chase and James, he liked to take his readers on unhurried excursions through the desert. The essential significance of the place, he notes in *The Southern Sierras of California*, is the opportunity for wholesome open-air activities in country "so different from other parts of the United States as to seem a foreign land." Day-trippers obviously charmed him. In light, inexpensive cars that could "climb anything and take hairpin curves with neatness and equanimity," they went knocking about the backcountry, picking flowers, "kodaking," and "tossing up jolly little meals by the wayside when that suited them, as it did at least twice a day." When opportunity arose, they bought milk and eggs at roadside ranches. When night overtook them, they lodged at country inns. "At the end of it all they would sell the car at a not unreasonable discount for wear and tear, as others had done before them."

Although gasoline pumps and repair shops were noticeably absent in the 1920s, automobiles did their best to shorten distances, taking people into all the countryside as trains never could. Difficulties aside, people were determined to "do" the desert, to witness all the delights of wilderness exploration. They must have the sand dunes, the lizards, and the cacti to add to their list of things which they had seen and others had not.

Into the village they came, goggles over their eyes, "dusters" over their dresses, waving maps, hankies, and hats. In a convulsion of obscene noises they came, bucking and banging out of the ruts, spewing sand and internal combustion over everyone—and thereby warning that a noisier era was on the way. The dogs, used to sleeping safely at noon in the middle of Main, barked at them furiously. Crowds of suicidal kids chased them through clouds of dust. Meanwhile, with what seemed to be calculated indifference, a few local characters stood by with mules left over from the previous era, hoping to make money off their tomfoolery.

Unfortunately, the idea of Palm Springs as a tourist destination was still a novelty to the world, largely because the drive in was by way of an old wagon road. Word reached the local politicians and that changed fast. First, the county crew realigned and widened the old road, putting the boulders and cacti in their place several paces beyond. Then they sloshed on a few inches of Desert Mix—a little asphalt mixed with a little cement mixed with a little clay—and went away chuckling up their sleeves. In short, this wasn't a good road; it still rose and dipped and curved far more actively than anyone wished. But at least it wouldn't blow away, and that was cause for celebration.

On the desert it is traditional to hold your celebrations outdoors: concerts under the stars, graduation ceremonies on the lawn, birthday parties beside the pool, the elderly sitting in the shade, the young in the sun. Nobody liked to upset tradition, but elemental forces were at work here, creating some concern that the village worthies might have to celebrate indoors. The sky lowered upon the village and continued to drop. But as luck would have it, the rain held off until the last guest had gone home. Then it came, in torrents, a real toad-strangler they would call it. The next day dawned in more rain, with more rain after that. What a mess: sky slumped overhead, mud and flood underfoot, the village dissolved in helpless anxiety, the mothers praying that none of the children would develop appendicitis or break an arm.

After days of rain, the mist gave the illusion of storm's end. Out came the flood stories, with everyone congratulating everyone else on facing the calamity with such fortitude. Out came the rainfall figures, two inches at one place, close to three at another. Beyond the backyard fences things looked far worse. Someone had been around and was able to report the details: power lines down; railroad tracks washed out; creeks swollen with leaves and pieces of trees; the Whitewater River running fast and dangerous, with great standing waves over ten feet high. And what about the new road? Well, it was gone, boys. I mean *gone*. No trace of it to be seen, an entire road, vanished.

* * *

In spite of the traffic—or what passed for traffic in the decade that followed—Palm Springs remained a modest place with much to be modest about. But now it wasn't quite so off the beaten track, and it was possible—just—to shop in town. Hoping to boost the village into a new era of prosperity, the village worthies went on a street renaming spree. Not wanting to chuck local history entirely, they canvassed the resident Indian population for suitable names. Then, list in hand, they walked up one street and down another—North, Lemon, Lime, Orange, Lawn, Park, Palm—and renamed them alphabetically after the Indians: Arenas, the long-distance runner (to look at him was to appreciate how easily that mindless phrase "a magnificent specimen" came into many a villager's head); Belardo, the date rancher and tribal *paha* (ceremonial assistant); Chino, the witch man, and at the age of 126 (by his reckoning), the oldest man alive in the United States; Saturnino, the cowpuncher; Segundo, the bathhouse manager. Few people outside the Coachella Valley have ever heard these proud old names, full of unlikely Spanish vowels. Yet the names are still here, and daily they enter nearly every conversation: "Take Saturnino west to Belardo, then go north to Arenas . . . "

Looking back on that gentle world, on those habitually sunny days of the thirties, we find the scheme of things wonderfully narrow. While the big news in the big newspapers was dense with cold hard images of bank failures, business closures, bread lines, and suicides, news at home was of Herbert Carpenter off on a quail shoot and Shelton Gray home from a gold hunt. A local bird whipped up more excitement at the *Desert Sun* when it won first prize in the national singing canary contest. Other columns detailed the doings of the churches, the endless social rounds of parties, the meetings of the Western Week committee, every item reported at tedious length and with eternal boosterism. And several corners of the *Sun* were always left open for the rounds of births and deaths. No reporter could write like that today, could use terms like "called by Death," "answered last summons," "gathered to his everlasting rest." Not that it mattered how they reported it, because the villagers always knew the news long before it was out.

A new decade arrived and with it, the unexpected blow of Pearl Harbor. No longer was the war something separate from village life. It was life itself, the start of real news, what the *Sun* had been waiting for. There was nothing to compare with it, the profound changes taking place as Uncle Sam grabbed desert property for the war effort.

Khaki jeeps and uniforms filled the streets—a night on the town for the boys stationed at Camp Young, fifty miles east of Palm Springs. Here on a windswept landscape, at once desert and deserted, the echo of artillery duels could be heard in the surrounding Chuckwalla Mountains as everything from tanks to sunglasses was tested in preparation for the North African campaign. What else they were doing out there in that stupefying expanse of tents the *Sun* couldn't say for fear of giving away war secrets.

The pilots from the Ferry Command made their own editorial contributions to the *Sun* when the army took over the tiny village airstrip and turned it into something its sportsmen-pilots wouldn't recognize: a sprawling transfer depot where planes fresh from factories on the West Coast stopped over for inspection before flying off to destinations and destinies unknown. "Here tonight, gone tomorrow," Wilberta "Ma" Lipps reported to the press. "Breakfast in Palm Springs. A late dinner in Kansas City." Although Lipps had not asked for nurturing duties beyond those common to any hotel owner in time of war, she obviously cared deeply for these lonely young pilots so in need of nurturing. She fetched them from the airport, cashed their checks, and ministered to their hang-overs, ripped trousers, and sunburns. She sent their telegrams, forwarded their mail, and held their laundry when they flew off for Kansas City, Montreal, Tampa, or wherever. "How," she wondered, "they are able with unerring skill to pilot their ships to their far destinations and yet are helpless to cope with missing socks, ties, fountain pens, and wrist watches, is one of the mysteries of life . . . As the drone of their planes dies away, I breathe a little prayer for them, well knowing, as they do, that their destiny is manifest."

The worst things can happen, and yet the world comes back to normal. Apart from the obvious horrors of warfare itself, peace brought an end to anxieties and separations, to cheerless Christmases and thankless Thanksgivings, to the weary rituals of rationing and salvaging, the *Sun* rousing its readers to do their part. Now reporters lapse into a weary silence, as far as one researcher can tell. "Village Takes War's End Calmly" was all the *Sun* had to say on that August day in 1945.

Which brings me to March 1946, when my father, Hugh E. Stephens, M.D., a latter-day health-seeker (emphysema plagued him all his adult life), moved us to Palm Springs: pop 7,157 according to the new census. Apparently we arrived just in time. The Community Desert Hospital had just opened for business, an event the *Sun* greeted with a "sigh of relief," for no longer would the police have to load accident victims into the "one-stretcher ambulance" and drive them "hell-bent for election" to Indio or Riverside, "while the victim's screams of pain mingled with that of the siren."

The newly arrived Stephens family also witnessed the first ever broadcast of the first ever radio station in Palm Springs. Actually we missed the exact moment, but again the *Sun* was there, making an important fuss while "the silver notes" of Joe Porretta and his band, broadcasting from the dance floor of the Colonial House, went "shimmering over 1340 kilocycles" of KCMJ. Suddenly you were out there, fox-trotting. That same evening, NBC's *Inner Sanctum* "hit the antennae of every radio set in the Village." Sound effects, having been developed into a veritable art form by this time, were what this show was really about: the ungodly creak of the door, the grim organ chords, the narratives featuring the most farfetched and downright impossible murder tales ever devised, punctuated with chortling villains, midnight shrieks, and grisly allusions that scared us kids out of our wits.

My dad's cousin Sallie, having moved here years earlier from Los Angeles, paved the way for our move from Santa

Barbara. Her realtor husband, Culver "Nick" Nichols, built my dad's small office on Palm Canyon Drive and sold him (for $16,500) the house with the red shutters in the (relatively) wind-free south end of town. My dad's profession automatically made him a respected citizen in town, professional men in those days being the embodiment of intelligence, training, self-reliance, and saintly dedication. At the same time, his reluctance to take up golf (what little leisure he allowed himself was spent in the company of a tennis racquet) made him socially suspect.

Issues of ancestry were never important to my dad, or therefore to me. But one evening, among the usual dinnertime clatter, he constructed our family tree, and in so doing passed along an intriguing fact about Cousin Sallie, namely, that her father was *the* Prescott "P. T." Stevens, Colorado cattleman turned Hollywood realtor turned Palm Springs developer. Stevens (who had married a Stephens just to confuse things) came to the village in 1912, purchased a thousand acres from the railroad—indeed, most of the land in the north end of town—and became one of the village's most active citizens, recognized on sight upon emerging from his long chauffeured Marmon limousine, the message "Palm Springs and Hollywood" scripted on the doors so he'd get a lot more recognition. Stevens stabilized the public water system and developed the first golf course, and thereby got his name in all the local history books. Unfortunately, he is remembered most as principal backer of the El Mirador Hotel. I say *unfortunately* because four years after its grand opening on New Years Eve 1927, the hotel failed, saddling Stevens with a burden of debt. With his last days on earth underway, he sold out to the bondholders. When it comes to founding fathers I can't help but feel somewhat disappointed.

Stevens passed to his reward but the El Mirador Hotel lived on, surviving the Depression relatively unscathed (it also survived the war as an army hospital and prisoner of war camp, a vast barracks of a place that matched the military mood of the airport). It would be misleading to call the El Mirador a hotel and leave it at that. It was a grandly pink affair with arches, pinnacles, balconies, a red tile roof, and a swimming pool that attracted celebrated guests from Hollywood, wowing them with five diving boards and a plate glass window for underwater breast-and-leg photography. Most remarkable was the bell tower, lost to a fire but faultlessly rebuilt, wherein two white guys calling themselves Amos 'n' Andy broadcast their hokey moralism, during which time the entire nation came to a halt to listen.

So there it is after all, that star-struck business I've tried to avoid in these pages because it's as overworked a topic as there is. Still and all, movie stars loomed large in village history, and their stories lent a particular patina to the place.

* * *

As far back as the real good old days of J. Smeaton Chase, the elements of Hollywood figured prominently in the perpetually amusing village. Palm Springs the Movie. Chase loved it, "the thrill of the real thing, flesh and blood (with paint and powder thrown in). In the last few years Palm Springs has become headquarters, so to speak, for Algeria, Egypt, Arabia, Palestine, India, Mexico, a good deal of Turkey, Australia . . . "

Flesh and blood, and a lot of movie-making in the old reckless sense. Imagine the scene: A caravan of large open motorcars discharges its load of heroes, villains, stunt men, camera crews, and extras—a wild and godless bunch quite capable of corrupting the village young. A man dressed in jodhpurs, leather boots, and puttees shouts "Action!" into a megaphone, and foreign legions march across the dunes, hell-for-leather posses trail bad men up the canyons, and whooping Comanches ambush stagecoaches at the pass.

Our desert also did itself proud in the role of antagonist, with frame after frame employing the theme of struggle. William de Mille recognized that role in *Heir to the Hoorah*. The story takes little effort to tell. The battered hero (played by Thomas Meighan), lost and slowly dying of thirst, reaches a water hole only to find it dry. Half-crazed by mirages, Meighan plods on, only to disappear into the heat haze. Slow fade-out. The End.

It's difficult to imagine our lush Indian canyons as an appropriate setting for *Heir*; it's the first place tourists want to see, the first place guides want to show. Except that it was filmed in August, in the days when the village was, in every sense of the word, a frontier, served by a little country store. There was no glamour of services, no ice within fifty miles. "The heat was so killing," reckoned de Mille in his autobiography, "that I didn't let Tom [Meighan] play up in rehearsal— just walked him through it to get camera composition and position, and also to be sure that the route he traversed was fairly clear of rattlesnakes, scorpions, centipedes and other items which might take an actor out of the proper mood."

In spite of the heat, or because of it, scene after scene progressed quickly right up to the end. As the camera cranked on, Tom's figure dwindled to a pinhead. Then it faded into the territory of myth. But scarcely had the director ordered

"Cut!" when a yelp came from whence the hero had faded, a cry "composed of pain, rage, surprise, disgust, and appeal." Fearing the worse, de Mille rushed his crew across the desert which, whatever else it contained, contained no sign of Tom Meigan. Then suddenly there he was, in the arroyo over which he had disappeared, sprawled bottomside down on a huge prickly pear cactus, his face contorted with pain. "He was keeping motionless but not quiet."

A flurry of outstretched hands reached down and lifted Meighan from his "seat of pain" to a "less penetrating resting place." They stretched him out flat, face down on the sand, well out of camera range. They clipped his trousers away. They plucked the cactus needles from his hindquarters. There is little else to tell. Meighan eventually recovered from his daylong surgery, but never from his embarrassment. As for de Mille, whenever he saw that particular film sequence, he felt an irrepressible urge to giggle.

How strange it is that in de Mille's time, studio luminaries and their retinue, unwillingly dragged to this offbeat location, took a liking to it and with the speed of a movie set transformed the gentle community before anyone quite realized what was happening. The "movies" (as early Hollywood called its film folk, as well as the product they produced) provided the village with outside money and bit parts for homegrown characters. In turn, the village made of the movies beloved celebrities. What they thought, what it was *thought* they thought, what they said, what it was *said* they said, what they did, what it was felt they *might* do, was an appealing way to fill up editorial space in the fledgling *Desert Sun*.

Ah, Palm Springs: the glitz, the glamour, the energy, the fun. *You're* from Palm *Springs*? I heard this throughout my teens, tone saying all. Back then, I had enormous gratitude for all those famc ¿s people who poured excitement into our lives. So wonderful to see them in the flesh, to stand for a moment in their spotlight. As I write this I see them once again: Red Skelton, Kirk Douglas, Cary Grant, Bobby Darin, Tab Hunter, John F. Kennedy, Gerald Ford, Timothy "turn on, tune in, drop out" Leary, Walt Disney, Bob Hope . . . so many. It mattered little whether the face represented a movie, a political office, an art, a science, or a scandal, the thrill of recognition provided conversation at school for an otherwise lost weekend.

You would be hard put to name a celebrity who didn't live in Palm Springs at one time or other. "Here was little Frank [Sinatra] when he first came out here, and he made his first million," recalls Prickly Pear architect Roger Williams. "And his idea—and he was a grocery clerk, and the son of a grocery store owner. And his idea was that if he ever had money he was going to build a big, beautiful Georgian mansion with columns and stone balustrades on it." In other words, architecture with a capital A, as Sinatra understood it, an extravagant landmark that would make the neighbors feel impoverished and small. Everyone would have hated it, and Sinatra's architects came to see it as a calamity to their careers. "We'd have been ruined right then and there." With as much tact as they could muster, they persuaded Old Blue Eyes to stick with the standard fat-cat design. Architecture, in other words, as a metaphor for the good life as it is locally understood. Into such a scheme, Sinatra's swimming pool, shaped like an amoeba, fit perfectly.

The current fashion among celebrities is to fix your villa, at fabulous expense, to the side of a mountain. It appears that for the sake of a view, some people are willing to gamble the whole investment, and perhaps life itself, on the slim hope that our segment of the San Andreas Fault will not move in a big way. On a mountainside called Southridge, the homes of Arnold Schwarzenegger and Sylvester Stallone overlook the vast gridded flatland—and thereby dominate it. Bob and Dolores Hope's multi-million-dollar dream house stands even higher. It's an altogether curious structure, a clear visual and social statement that has never been a neutral topic in town. Some people say it looks like the Anaheim Convention Center. Some say it looks like an extra-terrestrial invasion of the mountain. Hope's Folly they call it. The Volcano. The Mushroom. The Turtle-Top. Everyone agrees a thing like that takes over the mountain, and it takes the Georgian mansion metaphor several steps further.

Hope's house is 25,000 square feet of steel and glass, capped by a roof of ostentatiously gleaming copper. The scale is indicated by the living room; it seats three hundred guests. Hope's swimming pool, it is said, is shaped like Hope's profile. The person who says so is Shirley, and she ought to know because she works for the company that recently brought me up to date on celebrity homes.

Sometimes we locals miss things; think of the New Yorker who has never taken the ferry out to the Statue of Liberty. Well, it was about time for me to complete the Palm Springs experience. Although, to be honest, I have little interest in celebrity homes and even less interest in tours, which are, after all, more suited to tourists. Tour companies like large groups. They like herding them, lecturing them, counting them, scheduling their day, which always has something of an air of ritual to it, the timetable posted in the hotel rooms:

5:00 A.M. Wake-Up Call
5:45 A.M. Breakfast
7:00 A.M. Meet in Lobby.

Armed with box lunches, cameras, and sunscreen, they're off
to the celebrity homes today, the Indian canyons tomorrow,
the Living Desert (check out the Meerkat Cafe their guide-
book suggests), the Palapas Gardens (which they will entirely
take over), the air museum, the wind farms, a half hour here,
an hour there, a forced march of sight-seeing, with a perky
tour guide expounding, interpreting, hustling them back
aboard their air conditioned coach so they can get on to the
next place, and the next, until finally, blessedly, exhausted beyond caring *what* Palm Springs has to offer, they head back to
the hotel without really seeing Palm Springs at all. There
wasn't time.

Twenty of us boarded Shirley's bus that day, retired couples
mostly, in dreamy wintertime retreat; we had exchanged basic
information in the hotel lobby. Behind me sat two young
wives sprung from their hotel rooms for an afternoon's outing
while their husbands were at a housewares convention, discussing closet organizers and hide-away hampers. At the helm
was Shirley, retired realtor and grandmother of six. She was
heavy-set, the shoulders were square, the arms thick with the
unarguable strength of a prison matron. Her one meaty hand
gripped the steering wheel, her other, the microphone. Her
voice, husky from cigarettes and overuse, had kept the tone of
her New York roots, but you could tell it had been places.
"The first thing people want to know when they come to
Palm Springs is, Where are the movie stars? Do we ever get to
see any? Well, I do not guarantee a celebrity today, but I'll do

57

my best to find one. Yesterday I found Barry Manilow in his driveway. He was backing out, and he smiled and waved." Shirley gave us all this while avoiding a collision with a white Cadillac that had rushed at her suddenly from the left. It soon became apparent that Shirley did not leave a lot of time during her running commentary for scrupulous attention to traffic. Several times she had to drown out her own voice with indignant blasts of the horn.

After managing a remarkably deft turn off the highway, Shirley plied the quiet streets of the Old Movie Colony, a deeply romantic enclave of "our very best homes," many of which were considered mansions in the 1920s. The homes looked owned but not lived-in, as if their absentee owners had brought the decor to a high pitch then wandered away, bored.

On we rolled to the proud old-money neighborhood of Las Palmas, a stratosphere of Spanish-style homes, some of which take up entire blocks with their swimming pools, tennis courts, and clusters of guesthouses. Hurling her elderly bulk from side to side, Shirley pointed out the estates as if they were national shrines. "*That's* where Dean Martin lived before his divorce. *That's* where Kenny Rogers lived before he moved. *That's* where Dinah Shore lived before she died. *That's* the home of Barbara Hutton, the poor little rich girl who went wherever Cary Grant went. The shop-keepers tagged them Cash and Carry. Funny, huh?" Only one thing was indisputable: it was hard for Shirley to tell a joke a hundred times.

I cannot tell you how pleased we were to learn that the unsinkable Debbie Reynolds is still living here. At the twelfth or twentieth stop, I forget which, we were directed to lift our eyes to a hillside buried in scarlet bougainvillea. But what can you say about another stucco villa; it's another stucco villa and

58

that is that. After squelching a sudden hope that Ms. Reynolds would suddenly walk out her gate and invite the whole bunch of us in for iced tea, the lady from Cleveland slumped in her seat. "Debbie's very nice, you know." She could tell because she had seen her on the stage at Las Vegas.

Reciting movie titles and song titles and book titles, Shirley talked us happily up and down the narrow streets, summarizing lives at breakneck speed, making them sound all the more reckless and exotic. "Here's where Vicki Carr stayed when she was in town. Here's where Spiro Agnew stayed when he was in town and did not stay with Frank Sinatra. Here's where the Prince of Wales booked a room but did not stay when he stayed at the Walter Annenberg estate." With the pride of an owner, with sweeping waves of her microphone, she drew our attention to the house where Debbie Reynolds and Eddie Fisher spent their honeymoon, to the house where Eddie Fisher and Liz Taylor spent *their* honeymoon, to the house where Liz Taylor and Mike Todd spent *their* honeymoon, to the house where Liz Taylor and Mike Wilding spent *their* honeymoon. Obediently we followed her every gesture, took her star stories as gospel, these endless anecdotes culled from the society pages of our local press. After all, this is what we had come for. We wanted the marriages, the separations, the divorces of all of Hollywood's perfect couples.

The bus swung from curb to curb. Our mass swayed, tilted, and slid. Our heads rolled right, then left, then right. Out the delicately tinted windows we stared at the suggestion of roof lines behind miles of walls that the rich and famous had thrown around themselves to keep us from trespassing even visually. What secrets were they hiding? A marijuana patch? A movie great sunbathing in the raw? Oh, occasionally, when someone left a gate open, we got a glimpse of a deep, green courtyard with rare potted palms in the wall niches, a vignette so brief it was only tempting. "Beautiful home," said the man from Seattle, a comment he repeated at five-minute intervals all afternoon.

Beautiful indeed, but with a self-important showing of seclusion, a seclusion that suggested conflict rather than neighborly love, the iron fences cast in a pattern of spears, the walls posted with warnings of armed response, hidden mikes, and closed circuit cameras. The guard dogs not only warned of intruders but dealt with them. I pictured savage rottweilers bursting from their sheet-metal doghouses and lunging at the gates. Or in one case, a pair of fat, slothful Great Danes guided by a wildly-yapping poodle.

To judge from the speed at which we progressed through the rest of the tour, Shirley had already transferred her interest to the next group on her schedule. Nevertheless, we kept our heads covertly aswivel for Barry Manilow, Tammy Fay Bakker, Trini Lopez—I could go on, except that Shirley hung up her microphone and zoomed us back to the hotel, the traffic once again making way for our hooting-tooting grandmother. Presently, and quite remarkably, we came to a grinding halt in the parking lot, without a collision. By this time, I felt as if I had known Shirley—Shirl—all my life. In the last hour or so we had been through a lot together. Now that she had gone quiet, I could tell she was upset, that she had very badly wanted to show us a celebrity, so we wouldn't think she had made everything up. I sympathized with her disappointment but I did not share it. Indeed, most of us enjoyed the tour. For a few of us it was "okay" or "not bad." Only one of us found it far from what the "Where to go in Palm Springs" advertisement made it out to be. That settled, I dutifully purchased a picture postcard of Jean Harlow's gate and another of Elvis Presley's wall, planning to donate them both to the next starstruck tourist I met.

* * *

You gotta love them, the old movie greats. Even during the depths of the Depression, while most Americans were dipping into the bottom of whatever barrel they could find, celebrities swarmed the village, getting themselves into the local papers in tiresome numbers, the press doing the work of their publicists. Gambling was well within their interests and means. After recreating all day, having a healthy time of it under the sun, they liked to squash up close at night, hip to haunch with the underworld.

On the desolate outskirts of Palm Springs, in what is now incorporated Cathedral City, there were three gambling hideaways known by everyone through reputation and gossip. What looms first in the memories of the Prickly Pear pioneers is Frank Portnoy's Cove Club, a knockdown gangsterish place with a panel in the door that slid back to reveal a disembodied pair of glaring eyes. Second in memory is Earl Sausser's 139 Club, a "honky-tonk sawdust joint" that was defended by means of a guard turret on the roof, wherein a used-up prize fighter kept a watchful eye upon the proceedings, a Tommy gun cradled in his lap. And a third memory: the Dunes Club, a stucco palace owned and operated by Al Wurtheimer of Detroit's Purple Gang, a prosperous, if loose, confederation of gangsters who controlled almost everything criminal. One look at the Dunes, glowing like an Emerald City in that void of sandy desert, and you felt surely it had been built by mistake, had been intended for some other place altogether. For here was pure swank tricked out in Spanish tile, French windows, crystal chandeliers, soft blue carpeting, and great swaths of ivory brocade. Everything about the Dunes impressed: the long mahogany bar, polished to a glare; the felt-top tables where serious bettors shed hundred dollar bills; the dance floor where a string ensemble played the sentimental swing of the era; the elevated balcony, like in an opera house, where Dietrich, Cantor, Flynn, Bogart, Zanuck, and the Ritz Brothers, resplendent in black tie and gown, sat in gala display. In the sunken dining room—a luxury of linen and gilt-edged china—a maitre d' cruised the aisles with a pistol stuffed in his cummerbund, and tuxedoed waiters flourished platters of sumptuous à la dishes prepared by adept French hands.

Philip Boyd, who would become our first mayor, was present at the meeting when Wurtheimer proposed his idea of the Dunes, as if it were an enormous gift to the village, which indeed it was for the local businessmen. Plagued by the Depression and an ever-worsening American economy, many tourist-hungry hotels, unable to pay the interest on their loans, were facing foreclosure. In a Prickly Pear interview, Boyd recites from memory what Wurtheimer had to say:

> I will build a very handsome club, we'll have good food there, we'll have interesting music. And I will bring people from the east who know my activities in Detroit . . . And they'll fill your hotels. You will then be pulled out of this distress that you're in now . . . All I want you to do is not to complain to the county sheriff's department—the authorities—as to what we're doing. Let me handle that.

In return, Wurtheimer agreed to ban the local working stiffs from the back room, lest they blow a season's wages in an hour's play. He also promised to close the Dunes if the club's influence destroyed the village's "attractive features."

Absolutely. You tell me. I'll close down if you don't think I've brought you prosperity and attracted new people.

It all sounds more scandalous than it really was. But in fact, California was rife with illegal gambling, from floating casino ships anchored off Long Beach and Santa Monica to slot machines all over the state. Gambling was simultaneously enjoyed and despised, and the law was honored primarily in its breach and through the voluntary neglect of local authorities.

To his credit, the Riverside County district attorney, Earl Redwine, wanted to close the Dunes. Unfortunately, Sheriff Rayburn had the only law enforcement unit in the county, and he could not be persuaded to cooperate. Who could blame him? The hotel owners and most of the downtown merchants tacitly supported gambling for the sake of the tourist trade, and the local newspapers treated all three gambling clubs charitably in their columns. Oh, occasionally, when people were having too much fun, the old scolds, who never could get into the spirit of things in general and considered gambling a particular abomination, would precipitate a raid. In which case, regular payments to Sheriff Rayburn ensured that word was passed along well in advance. By the time the law showed up, the party was long over.

Because of the corruption that came out of the Dunes, makeshift gambling cropped up all over the village, a little craps, a little blackjack, a little poker, and a whole lot of slot machines. The feeling was difficult to miss as the usual people raised the usual objections in the local press. This from H. Bedford-Jones:

Our children cannot go to the Dunes, but here they can gamble freely day and night under the auspices of Riverside County. The average workman or clerk finds the Dunes a bit beyond him; but he can sink his pay-check quicker in the drug store than he ever could in the corner saloon.

This from Frank "Pop" Shannon:

I am unalterably opposed to slot machines. I never put a nickel in one of them in my life and never expect to because I know they are not made for the man who puts the nickels in, but for the man who takes the nickels out. I believe they have very dire consequences for young people who get the slot machine habit.

This from Hobart Garlick:

I have not retired so far from the local battle ground that I wouldn't take up the fight to drive [slot machines] out of Palm Springs. They encourage the petty gambler who cannot afford to lose—but who does lose and must either skip paying his bills or resort to petty pilfering to keep the slot machines busy.

At some point, the village fathers stood up as one and asked Wertheimer to fulfill his promise to close the Dunes. His reaction followed totally predictable lines. Boyd remembers the moment exactly:

He rose angrily and said, "to hell with all of you! I control the county law enforcement and I'm too heavily invested to stop now." It was a most unfortunate situation.

And so it went. Or would have, had it not been for Earl Warren, who, you will remember, rose through the ranks—racket-busting district attorney in Oakland, three-term governor of our state—until he became chief justice of the U.S. Supreme Court. According to his biographers, Warren was incorruptible. As a conservative Republican, he was very much for God and motherhood and very much against sin, crime, and what he considered the parasitic industries. "I must confess," he notes in his memoirs, "to an ingrained bias against commercialized gambling."

So, after trying unsuccessfully to induce Sheriff Rayburn to close the Dunes, Warren did the job himself. "The taking of the place was an exciting experience," he writes, "but a raid is a raid no matter how large or difficult, and it should be sufficient to say that this gambling house was permanently closed." As for Wertheimer, he was convicted of maintaining a gambling establishment, fined eight hundred dollars, and sentenced to the county road camp, where, in deference to his old age and poor health, he did his time in the kitchen, peeling spuds for the chain gang. After enduring months of humiliation, he was then convicted of tax evasion, and his infamous Dunes, with all its elegant fixtures and furnishings, was sold at public auction. When a fire closed the Dunes for good, nobody bothered to look for the cause. Such things were best left uninvestigated.

Years after the ashes settled, the lives of Wurtheimer and Warren converged again when out of the proverbial blue they found themselves seated side by side on a commercial flight from Los Angeles to Sacramento. Wurtheimer, having recognized the governor, turned in his seat and introduced himself. "You drove me out of California," he said, "but there are no hard feelings because I am established in Nevada now, and my gambling is perfectly legal."

After Warren's raid on the Dunes (this was not Sheriff Rayburn's finest hour), with no bustle of ceremony, the slot machines disappeared—the dozens in operation and the dozens still in their shipping crates—taking a load off everyone's mind. Unlike the Dunes, the 139 Club met an honorable end as the Humane Society's thrift shop. The Cove also represents a triumph of recycling, surviving today as the Elk's Lodge, where bingo in the back room keeps tradition alive.

* * *

In spite of the action, as gamblers like to say—or the sudden lack of it—Palm Springs was bound to grow after the Second World War. Conditioned air made the desert far more bearable. Commercial air travel made it far more accessible to the rest of America and beyond. From 1945 to 1948 Palm Springs doubled in size, more than doubled from 1950 to 1960, more than tripled from 1960 to 1995. Actually, growth was measured in months rather than years, and it never took a review of population figures to be aware of it. Crime and smog increased. Supermarkets became tangibly more crowded, highways annoyingly more jammed. You got used to it, of course, as usual. Either you adjusted or you went crazy. There was no sense in protesting the disappearance from the city of yet another pleasant little rectangle of wildflowers. No one questioned the desirability of growth. Everyone was for it. They campaigned for it. They advertised, and the voices of the advertisers blended with the voices of the press. Growth, growth, went the mantra. Any city not growing was bound to die.

Today's promoters and their ilk are still at it, still playing on the obsessive search for paradise. Consequently, twenty years hence, population figures for the Coachella Valley are expected to jump from 318,000 to twice that number, if the estimates of the experts are correct; the *Desert Sun* gives us the news in long columns and big headlines. I can only guess what it will be like. I turn to my mother, hoping that she might know something comforting that I do not.

THREE

Slowly through the Canyon

On the picture screen you've seen it represented as the African Congo or the South Seas. In magazines and newspapers you've found it featured in illustration and advertisement; and from the moment of your arrival in Palm Springs you encounter The Canyon "done" in oils and watercolors and sketches. You find it lithographed and photographed and superimposed on every conceivable type of gift item and gadget.

—PALM SPRINGS VILLAGER, APRIL 1949

*J*UST MINUTES FROM the outdoor cafes and T-shirt shops of downtown Palm Springs, South Palm Canyon Drive narrows to a two-lane blacktop, then terminates at the entrance to three Indian canyons. They are all well worth a visit, for here lies a far stretch of backcountry, of cactus mesas, surprise oases, and little creeks that somehow manage a few waterfalls before meandering out through the sand. The scenery itself is not the half of it. The canyons shelter far more ghosts and myths than anyone's memory can span.

Concealed in a steep-walled granitic gorge, Palm Canyon, my destination on this warm April morning, splits the San Jacinto and Santa Rosa Mountains along the (thankfully) long-dormant Palm Canyon Fault. I find that with a few field guides and the knowledge of a friend or two, it's fairly easy to name what can be seen there. But the geology, although it's evident, sticking up there in the air, is exceedingly complex, horribly tedious, and a great burden on my memory.

In the seat beside me is a knapsack packed with sweatshirt, trail snacks, cameras, wildflower lenses, and half a dozen rolls of film. I have thrown in a raincoat, even though every joint in my body says no rain today. Otherwise my attire is casual, pretty much what most women would wear if they didn't have to go to the office: khaki hiking shorts, an increasingly off-white T-shirt, and a pair of Nike sneakers that already have seen too many trails.

Stop! demands the big red sign on the fence. There are other signs to read—rules of canyon etiquette that always make me feel like an unwelcome guest who cannot quite be trusted to behave. I am forbidden to camp or to smoke. Alcohol and firearms are forbidden. Pets are forbidden, loud radios and bicycles. Cars not out of the parking lot by six o'clock will be towed away at owner's expense—no exceptions. There are no fewer than half a dozen signs posted throughout the canyons reminding you of this.

The snowy mountaintops are on the melt. It's that kind of morning, typical to our desert in spring, sunny with just an edge of coolness to the breeze. It's a great day, everything right with the world, even as another El Nino storm is poised over the Pacific, about to make landfall in Los Angeles. Before leaving the house, I had caught the weather channel. The barometric pressure had sunk to a stormy 29.4.

The season has been wet, and California dreamers are wondering when it will end. The jokes about El Nino, so common last fall, were stilled in February as reporters resorted to the thesaurus, trying to give adequate weight to storms that blew in, barreled in, rammed, ripped, roared, slammed, swept, soaked, swiped (savagely). *Rain* and *fall* just wouldn't do it. Meanwhile, as wave after stormy wave swamped the southland, as cliffs crumbled into the surf and infuriated commuters fiddled in vain for a higher speed on their windshield wipers, those of us living in Palm Springs, protected by the mountains, experienced the gentler side of El Nino: some light rain, some sun, some more light rain. I, for one, never want or expect a winter of total sunshine. Desert landscapes photograph best in the soft gray moodiness only clouds can produce.

Dressed in a bold floral smock and rubber flip-flops, my Indian hostess for today emerges unsmiling from the tollbooth. With an absolute minimum of conversation, she takes my entrance fee. Given that she speaks English, fluent English, as do all members of the Agua Caliente Band, I wonder at her reserve. But perhaps she has seen too many visitors come and go, some of whom have come to the Indian canyons only to see the Indians, noble savages in pagan undress, living in wigwams, close to the bone—an absurdity that has demanded from her no end of explanation.

We have, most of us local hikers, other images of the canyon, and after parting with six dollars, I am allowed to drive on in search of these wonders. Instinctively I hug the shoulder, a sandy edge littered with warnings of steep climbs and blind curves. Honk Horn. Low Clearance. Respect speed limit, paleface. Speed limit observed, I climb steeply and curve blindly to road's end at Hermits Bench, the jumping-off place for hikes into Palm Canyon.

On this Monday morning the parking lot is empty. Well, almost empty. Willie Boy, the parking lot coyote is here, a jittery creature who stays alive on the doughnuts Millie Fischer hands out, tailings, I imagine, from her own hearty breakfast. Millie Fischer, she with the freckles and girlish gray braids, is part Choctaw and part Cherokee, or so she claims. Her family owns the souvenir hut on Hermits Bench, and she can usually be found in the adjoining patio, surrounded by a dusty medley of beads, silver jewelry, and leatherwork, any number of which she might be tempted to part with for a price. I don't question Millie's good intentions, but feeding coyotes isn't good for them. It's a kindness likely to be repaid by bites on the hand, at which point the Fish and Game swat team will certainly be called in.

Today Willie Boy appears to have better things to do in his other, private life of stealth and plunder. Knowing himself watched, he trots off, stops to stare back at me, trots off again, stops again. Then abruptly he changes sex and squats, leaving enough scent to tantalize the resident males who will get wildly excited over this otherwise unremarkable patch of ground.

Hermits Bench looks like any other makeshift parking lot, except for the unexpected vista, a grand view that covers so much ground you can never get it all into one photograph however far back you stand. In 1917 this was home to young William "Peter" Pester, a minor folk hero who was called a hermit for good reason. His hair hung in hermit fashion over his shoulders, with a blond beard thrown in for good measure. He wore a monk's robe—when he wore anything at all—cut from what looked like a feed sack. He led a good life, simple, primitive, and poor, in a hut built solidly of palm logs. Life for Pester was a neat simplicity. For him clocks had not been invented, and time, as we understand it, did not exist. When it was dark he went to bed and when it was light he got up, with nothing much in between, no appointments, no commit-ments, no ambitions, no taxes, no debts, and only the smallest of cares and wants. Who has not dreamed of this, the canyon paradise?

Pester lived alone and so isolated that the burdens and suf-ferings of the world could not reach him. Well, that isn't com-pletely true. Almost daily he suffered the intrusion of the curi-ous few, to whom he sold arrowheads, walking canes, and postcards that gave dietary advice (yes: fruits and vegetables, no: red meat and sugar). He put on a good show, this hermit, posing for their cameras as Nature Boy at His Dinner and Na-ture Boy Reading the Bible and when the mood moved him as the Savior Himself with Robe and Staff. But he's really a college professor, went the talk around town. A lawyer, a mil-lionaire. He's stinking rich. Reeking with money. All his life he's been used to having everything he ever wanted, so noth-ing interests him anymore. He likes to see how many things he can do without—food, people, clothes, books, everything.

German by birth, Pester came out of the blue, was widely visible for a time, then simply faded away. If his story had been set in the Rockies, it would have ended with an eccentric old man dying alone in a mountain cabin. But this was Palm Springs after all. And in 1938, after 442 of its registered voters voted to incorporate themselves as a city, the newly-elected fathers, split on other issues, became united and strong on this one. They were familiar with hermits and hermits were not their heroes. And while no one had actually come out and complained about Pester, the feeling was difficult to miss. He was gay, explained a woman to the editor of *Desert Magazine*. *Gay*? Now where could she have picked up that term back then? Did it bear a relationship to the modern meaning of the word? I reach for my Webster's: "4. Inclined to the dissipations of society. Licentious. Loose. Leading an immoral life." In an era bedeviled by undue concern for morality, Pester had no lively hope of escaping (one almost wants to write *persecution*) from people with a sense of high social purpose.

Determined as I am to solve village mysteries, I have little else to tell. History of the footloose type can be distressingly vague. Although hardly anybody knew anything about Pester, the rumors continued. He's living in Bermuda Dunes, they said, laid low, humiliated. He died of tuberculosis in a Nevada sanitarium, an unchanged creature to the end. He's living in Thousand Palms with his new wife, but for whose good influence he would have certainly ended up in prison.

With a few tricks of the eye—block out Millie Fischer's patio and the portable outhouses—Hermits Bench is pretty much as Pester left it. Block out the thatched-roof hut where a safari guide runs hikes for visitors who feel they ought to be guided. Block out the souvenir hut where you walk the aisles more for entertainment than need. "I could look at those things for hours," a German woman once told me, referring to the scorpions entombed in lumps of plastic, their stingers arched over with menace.

Insect souvenirs, for those who wanted them, were available as far back as 1900. George Wharton James, sharp-eyed chronicler of the period, found the industry fascinating, and was sure we would too:

> Gathering curious insects by the thousands, putting them
> through a process of taxidermy and merchandising them
> for the edification of curiosity seekers is one of the most
> unique developments of life in the far west. The head-

quarters of this remarkable industry is located in Pasadena, California, and from an unpretentious and entirely experimental beginning several years ago, the business has expanded into immense proportions, over ten thousand bugs, insects and snakes are disposed of each year, yet the demand exceeds the supply.

The stock in trade came by way of young boys, most of whom entered into the "spirit of the chase" with great enthusiasm, the "financial proceeds" being considerable: five cents for centipedes; two cents for tarantulas, tarantula hawks, and scorpions; considerably more for trapdoor spiders.

> The search . . . is carried on systematically, and the rock clothing of Mother Earth is tossed about and disheveled with a most deliberate unconcern. No stone or boulder is passed without being rolled over . . . When these gruesome anthropoids [*sic*] have passed through the process of taxidermy, they are pinned on boards and placed in the sun to dry, just like so many trays of raisins.

When sufficiently cured, the insects were mounted on cards or arranged under glass paper weights and sold for two bits.

Besides gruesome arthropods, the souvenir hut on Hermits Bench also stocks a wholly unimaginative collection of palm tree postcards, palm tree place mats, palm tree T-shirts, palm tree key-rings, palm tree coffee table books, palm tree everything to prove that you've been here. Because whatever else Palm Canyon is, it is most of all palm trees. *Washingtonia filifera* they are called botanically, and there are over twenty-five hundred of them growing here, unplanned and haphazard, utterly wild and unpruned. There are palm trees to the left of you, palm trees to the right: lusty seedling palms with unopened fans, stout middle-aged palms with floor-length skirts, grand-father palms with naked, charred trunks, thriving veterans of countless fires. "It was the medicine men who burned the palm trees," Francisco Patencio tells us,

> so that they could get good fruit. The bugs [palm borer beetles] that hatched in the top of the palm trees, they made the tree sick, and no fruit came. After the trees were set afire and burned, the bugs were killed and the trees gave good fruit. Now that the medicine men are gone, the worms are taking the flowers, the green fruit, and the ripe fruit. There are so many things that it is too much to write it all. It would make too many books.

The fruits cannot be called dates; they are more like small berries no bigger than coffee beans, an exaggerated pit surrounded by a thin sweet skin. The Indians liked them well enough, or at any rate used them for food. Apparently the coyotes like them too; their scat is packed with seeds from which new palm trees will readily sprout.

Above the fruited clusters, the crowns of fronds form a canopy where robins and finches sing. Hooded orioles pull the curled fibers off the fronds to weave into baskets for their young. The dead fronds remain on the trunk throughout the life of the palm, forming a straw-yellow skirt that trails to the ground and creates prime habitat for bats, spiders, and snakes.

The hiker's way down to the palms is by a switchback cut across the base of Hermits Bench. From there, the most heavily used trail turns as the creek turns, hooking around boulders and idling beside swamps of cattails. For five hundred years, if not a great deal longer, this was home to the Cahuilla Indians, the first families of Palm Springs, the bluest of the blue bloods.

I don't kneel down to kiss the ground, but I stoop to pick up a candy wrapper.

* * *

In an amateur way, I have explored bits and pieces of Cahuilla history, beginning with the mid 1700s, when the Spanish Catholics came this way. Although the mission system itself did not extend east of the San Jacinto Mountains, the mission influence spread throughout our Coachella Valley, as evidenced by Francisco Patencio. As a child, he remembered his elders talking about the padres, how they were good men but were kept so busy tending their missions—the orchards, fields, and vineyards, the cattle, horses, and sheep ("so many of them"), the villages ("so many to feed, so much to be done")—they had little time to learn the Cahuilla language. So they took as assistants Indians who had learned Spanish, the *Kis-se-an-o*, the first Christian Indians.

> Even though the Indians were of their own race of people, many of these *Kis-se-an-o* men were hard and cruel . . . They it was who worked the Indians hard, and punished them. The Indian people are slow to learn different ways. They were not used to working at one thing all day. If they ran away, they were brought back and punished for it . . . The Indians thought they had learned to suffer, but now they learned it all—there was no more to know. The *Kis-se-an-o* became more and more cruel. They punished and murdered until whole tribes were wiped out.

This explains why Cahuilla fathers packed up their families and fled to the safety of Tahquitz Canyon, to the milder neighborhood of the mountain lion and rattlesnake.

From this place they could see below. They watched for strangers coming, and hid their children in the caves and cracks of the cliffs. They became like hunted animals searching for a safe place to hide their young.

Slavery it was, literal, hopeless, and shameful in our eyes, yet such was the mission system until Mexico threw off her allegiance to Spain, dismantled the missions, and set their Indian dependents adrift. But by now the Indians had lost the skills central to their ancestors' free-roaming life, and the land that had supported their ancestors now belonged to the strong-armed rancheros.

The Indians in their own country had no place to go. Their lives were dead like the dry mustard with the empty birds' nests in winter time.

Even more disastrous were the great epidemics that killed uncounted numbers of Indians in the following decades, the Old World diseases for which the medicine men with their steam baths and cold plunges were no match. No wonder Mahlon Fairchild lost his urge to linger in our desert; the scene was too sad:

The weather was very hot; children with skins spotted with the disease . . . would be sprinkled with water ejected from the mouths of the squaws to cool them off . . . During the short time I was there a score or more infants died . . . Generally the Indian huts were made of stout posts about five feet high with sides and roof thatched with boughs and coarse grass. Into several of these I saw them pile infant corpses with clothing and various other things and set them afire.

As disease decimated the Cahuilla population, an over-whelming force of settlers were about to diminish their lands. Indian Agent Colburn picks up the story:

> Now white men have set up claims of more or less valid character upon almost every acre of these lands and they are liable to be taken away unless there is strong and energetic action taken by the Government . . . That such lands have been held by Indians and cultivated by Indians counts nothing more than if they had been only homes for grasshoppers and coyotes.

Lo, the poor Indians! Never have the sins of our forefathers come home to roost with such irony as in Palm Springs. Nobody even knew where the place was in 1876 when, after decades of drafted but abandoned legislation, President Ulysses S. Grant handed over all the red squares of the checkerboard to the Agua Caliente Band of Cahuilla Indians. What was he thinking? This small forgotten band now owns every other section, that is, fully *half* of Palm Springs—for a mile you're on the reservation, then you're off, then you're on again, then you're off again . . . It is indeed an awkward arrangement that plagues city hall to this day. Right and proper, I have decided. Because in the beginning the Indians owned all of Palm Springs, in their heads. If nature did not draw lines, government certainly did. "What is reservation?" Patencio asked.

> That is not our language. That is white man's language . . . My people, they do not move. Always they live in one place. Only they go for the seed at harvest—only to be gone a short time. My people we love the place where we are born . . . My people could not live without their

homes, their gardens, their lands. This broke their hearts, to be moved about.

How precious and remote that aboriginal world now seems, that way of life so little heeded in today's complex world, even by the Cahuilla descendants themselves. (But do we arrive at the Indian canyons in prairie bonnets and flowing homespun?) Very soon their culture will be just another part of American folklore, treasured because it is folkloric. God knows what wealth of pragmatic botany will perish, has already perished, not just what grasses made good baskets, but also what was edible by a stretch of the hungry imagination. It seems that the secrets of plant powers yielded themselves readily to the Cahuillas, they who knew more about nature than the naturalists did, because they knew it in their lives, moment to moment. They knew that creosote leaves relieved coughs, that greasewood twigs steeped in tea produced "vomit and bowel relief," that buckwheat flowers soothed eyes made sore by the smoke of cooking fires. Add to these complaints mild fevers and occasional rheumatism, and you generally have the scope of Cahuilla pathology before Europeans introduced the great epidemics.

But there's hope. Even as today's Cahuillas embrace the existing system, the supermarkets that bring us toaster strudel and cheese in a spray can, a few diehard devotees remain committed to keeping tradition alive. For old times' sake, they serve their scrambled eggs topped with yucca blossoms and their Cream of Wheat topped with chia seeds. They harvest pinyon cones in traditional harvesting areas; then they cure them in a non-traditional microwave oven.

In theory at least, the Heritage Festival, held every April at the entrance to the canyons, is a more serious attempt to revive the old ways. In practice, it's a cultural jamboree organized for tourists who have gained their stereotypic impressions of Indians through Western novels and movies. But if it isn't always genuine, it is almost always fun. Here are the Apache Spirit Dancers, half-crouched, muscles bunched, sweeping the air with their primitive spears, in effect playing caricatures of themselves. A Sioux chief is no more than a hop-step away. Under a load of feathers and beads, he lifts our scalps with piercing cries, causing some backward shuffling in the front row. Now come the Cahuilla Indians dressed not in feathers and beads but in blue jeans, bolo ties, and ball caps. Looking off into the middle distance—not bored or evasive, just detached, free of the festival events, the chile cook-off, the petting zoo—they sing in the old language the old songs that once took a week of nights to sing, their voices rising unmemorably, their words containing gulps and glottal stops for which there are no symbols on my computer. They sing about the birds and the migration of the birds, about the people and the migration of the people, the songs themselves taking flight across the dusty fairgrounds. Although their performance appears ordinary, it's real enough and obviously deeply felt. And it never fails to move me more than is good for composure. I look around to see if my reaction is shared. If it is, there is no visible trace.

Here in the canyons, despite freelance archeologists ravaging the sites, authentic Cahuilla history still shows its dim mark in the form of arrowpoints, pottery sherds, and shell beads. You can, if you like, poke your toe in a hot mineral spring that once healed a hunter's weary bones. Go nosing around the ancient village sites, and where you would expect bare rock you'll find zigzags and concentric circles pecked through the dark patina. You'll find rock shelters with blackened ceilings where women in gossipy groups organized their busy days around a smoky fire. You'll find large flat grinding rocks where they mortar-and-pestled the beans of mesquite, a thorny, twisted tree that still grows wild in these canyons (the beans hang in clusters, a good crop almost bending the branches to the ground). As the mortar holes wore deeper and wider, the grains of iron pyrite in the mesquite-bean mush corroded their teeth, those of the elderly worn to stubs.

Even without the history, the canyons have always drawn crowds. Early in the twentieth century, various efforts to create a national monument out of Palm, Murray, and Andreas Canyons culminated in a congressional bill that was signed into law. That the canyons were owned by the Indians and not for sale was apparently deemed unimportant. Indeed, once the tribe *was* consulted, the idea died a rapid death. There was no question that the canyons were valuable to the tribe, as livestock pasture, as a source for traditional foods and medicines, as a sanctuary with historical and spiritual meaning, and that the government's offer of $22,000 for all three canyons was clearly chicken feed. And to make doubly certain that people understood just whose canyons these were, the tribe built a tollgate and began charging admission.

Equally interested were developers; they took a look at the canyons and misread them as land ready for development. To which the tribe responded with the weary echo: "We just want to be left alone on our own lands." Except that in 1965, when Walt Disney and Roy Rogers looked at Palm Canyon and decided it lacked only a museum and a hotel to complete and preserve the cowboy-Indian image, the tribe was "most happy to listen to anybody who has ideas for the canyons." Happily, nothing has taken hold. In fact, all three canyons, although still owned by the tribe, now fall under the newly-created Santa Rosa and San Jacinto Mountains National Monument. Apparently the canyons can be allowed to remain—as they were and as they are—without damage to profits, that is, just about the way nature wants them to be.

* * *

If you are hiking west from the mouth of lovely Palm Canyon, the hardly less lovely Murray Canyon comes next. The trail up Murray follows the creek, first one bank then the other, and a dozen times within a mile you must either ford the creek or cross it on risky boulders. But it's well worth the effort if only to visit the Seven Sisters, a series of scrambling cascades that nearly did me in. The climb is so steep you go up on all fours—and quickly learn to inspect each handhold for ants, cactus joints, and dozing rattlesnakes.

Murray Canyon was named for Dr. Welwood Murray who was not a real doctor. The man most often mentioned when discussing Murray is Judge John Guthrie McCallum who was not a real judge. In the Old West a title was useful when it came to gaining respect.

While growing up in Palm Springs, I had only the vaguest notion about who these two men were, and what, exactly, they had done. Although photographs of McCallum suggest he might have philosophized for a living, his voice coming from deep inside his wild white beard, in fact he was a San Francisco attorney turned agent for the Bureau of Indian Affairs, that long arm of the Interior Department charged with promoting the welfare of American Indians. In 1884, hoping to give the breath of life to his son Johnny, whose tubercular face already showed signs of an early death, McCallum moved his family first to Banning, then on to the small Indian village of Agua Caliente, later called Palm Springs. On eighty acres in what is now the Tennis Club area, he built a little L-shaped adobe home. Or rather, he directed Cahuilla artisans to build it for him, using bricks they made from the mud that surrounded their hot mineral spring. Ignoring the stubborn realities of the desert climate, McCallum then directed the planting of grapes, figs, apricots, citrus fruit, and a variety of melons—perfect lines of green stitched against the foot of the mountain.

That McCallum was possessed by the fever of speculation goes without saying. Only a speculator would dream of creating a colony of snug family ranches from practically nothing but climate and sand. As a speculator, he had come to the right place at precisely the right time, inasmuch as the Southern Pacific Railroad was eager to sell its granted land. Desert country it was, hospitable to cholla and little else, miles and miles of it going for $2.50 an acre. Seizing the moment, McCallum bought six thousand acres; they would surely be worth something someday. The ground under his feet could be paced out in dollars and cents.

All successful colonies require a reliable water supply. So again calling upon the apparently limitless supply of cheap Indian labor, McCallum built a ditch nineteen miles long, an open canal lined with cobblestones, bridged with wooden trestles, and fed by gravity from the Whitewater River, a mere stream in the best of times. However improbable, however primitive, it worked.

Now a general store with a post office was needed for his

colony to be. With this in mind, he refurbished a small room in a small building and stocked it with a rattlebag of merchandise: hay, bailing wire, tobacco, a pair of boots, perhaps, a few boxes of gingersnaps, cans of this and sacks of that, everything stacked every which way in every odd spidery corner. The post office at the far end (it was simply a box with eight dusty cubbyholes, if you want to get technical) only magnified the impression that the store didn't give a damn if it survived the next windstorm. But it was the only store in town. In every sense, it *was* the town,

In order to promote a place you have to mention a hotel. Raise a hotel, so the premise goes, and guests will come— McCallum had it all figured out. Some of his theories must have sounded untenable, if not actually weird, but there's something horribly contagious about enthusiasm. There's no other way to explain it, why old Welwood Murray, whose retirement plans did not include owning a hotel, found himself pressed into service as a hotelier. Hence he sold his Banning ranch, tore his wife from family and friends, and moved to what was basically a small Indian village.

On a five acre lot adjacent to the hot spring, Murray pitched a long, rambling hotel "of his own design." Land was cheap, and half a dozen rooms in a row were better than as many piled one above the other. Mrs. Murray, who was handicapped by overweight and "sweated a lot," would find it easier to go through a doorway than up a flight of stairs.

That settled, he turned his attention to landscaping his creation with slips and roots shipped in from romantic places all over the world. Especially trees, trees that would give him the illusion of being back in his greener, more orderly Scottish homeland. Murray was mad about trees. He loved them. He understood them. He cared for them as if they were his—I'm tempted to say *children*.

So the Palm Springs Hotel—No Camping Allowed came into being. It was the first hotel on the first street in Palm Springs. Somebody was going to do the thing and it happened to be Welwood Murray. In a photograph taken in the 1890s, we see him standing in the dusty courtyard of the hotel, a sparrowy man, his hands brown as onionskin. In a consciously relaxed pose, he represents the emblem of leisure life. Except that he looks unwell, as if a gust of wind would undo him. The pouches of flesh beneath his eyes look bruised. The flesh over his cheekbones is translucent and frail. For whatever reason, he is wearing not his usual skullcap and frock coat, but a buttoned-up cardigan that slumps from his shoulders and trousers that look like they would fall if he sneezed.

But in fact Murray lived to a ripe old age, in defiance of his enemy, consumption. All through the Big Flood and the terrible deadness of the Big Drought, he persevered, making money off the invalids. Pleasure for Murray was holding court over his guests. He could give the kind of performance that can be powerfully effective if the words are even half well-chosen, and you needn't doubt for a moment that Dr. Welwood Murray chose his words exceedingly well. He was an educated man, full of fine theories, whether you wanted to hear them or not. His explanations were long and tortuous, and often subject to passionate dispute. But as a rule you rarely interfered with his views; he was the undisputed authority on just about anything you would want to throw out for discussion. He knew everything. And he had been everywhere. And he liked to expound on his travels, exhausting Britain, then moving on to France, then Italy, then Turkey, a country that he had not actually visited, but that didn't stop him.

Even more pleasurable for hotelier Welwood Murray was playing host to such notables as George Wharton James, a hotel regular; and Charles Warren Fairbanks, Theodore Roosevelt's vice president; and Fanny Stevenson, widow of Robert Louis. ("Wonderful cures of tuberculosis have taken place here," she wrote to a friend. "If I had only known of Palm Springs in my Louis' time.") As for the visit of Helen Hunt Jackson, a stretching of the truth local historians have gladly repeated, it never took place. Nevertheless she was able to report that "there is in this desert one reservation called Agua Caliente . . . all barren, desert land with only one spring in it. These desert Indians are wretchedly poor, and need help perhaps more than any others in Southern California."

Jackson, you may remember, was the outspoken rebel who devoted the last years of her life to the American Indians, championing their cause against the American government. Her *Century of Dishonor*, dramatically bound between blood-red covers, was essentially a massive legal brief about the violation of their rights, a compilation of raw facts and figures that was greeted with an almost audible silence (upon its publication she had sent a copy, at her own expense, to every member of Congress). In contrast, her novel *Ramona* called such nationwide attention to their mistreatment, it has been dubbed a California *Uncle Tom's Cabin*. Never in her wildest dreams did Jackson imagine the furor and controversy this trite romance would create, or the tide of tourism it would unleash when *Ramona* devotees decided that they simply had to see Ramonaland for themselves: the orange groves "dark and glossy like laurel"; the air "delicious, languid, semi-tropical," filled with hummingbirds, butterflies, and birds; the creeks "always full of music"; the jagged tops and spurs of the San Jacinto Mountains, shining "like the turrets and posterns of a citadel built of rubies"—lofty stuff at best. If nothing else, *Ramona* and *Ramona* souvenirs and *Ramona* ballyhoo of all sorts contributed greatly to Southern California's image of itself and the nation's image of Southern California. And it brought in, by conservative estimates, fifty million dollars in tourist revenue.

The greatest pleasure of all for hotelier Welwood Murray was playing host to John Muir, he of the forested mountains and alpine lakes. John Muir? Coming to Palm Springs? In the dead of summer? Yes indeed. The stationmaster had sent the news, the bush telegraph in action. Muir was expected that very afternoon, along with his two daughters, Wanda and the younger Helen, whose lungs might benefit from the hot dry climate (this health-seeking metaphor can't be pushed too strongly). Imagine the frantic scene: the guest cottages must be readied—floors swept and mopped; pitchers filled with fresh water; wicks trimmed in the lamps; bowls, towels, and soap set on the washstands; baskets of fruit set on the bedside tables. Matronly Mrs. Murray was at pains to say how very dreadful it would be, all that dismal housekeeping in the hundred-degree heat. But it must be done, and done quickly. This called for outside help.

In a "paroxysm of haste" Dr. Murray dashed across the road to the reservation and returned with Ramon, "a stalwart young Indian," and Ramon's wife, Amada, "gowned in a voluminous calico mother-hubbard." Helen Lukens Gaut, a guest at the hotel during Muir's visit, sized up the situation for the local *Villager*. Handing out brooms, mops, and buckets, Murray then ordered the Indian couple to "exterminate the superflu-ous accumulation of dirt." The good doctor, Gaut explained, liked to familiarize the Indians with the niceties of the English language.

Ms. Gaut could have written volumes about Muir's visit, daily, until they stopped her. The impulse to write things down is peculiarly compulsive, and inexplicable to those who do not share the compulsion. Taking up her pen at the long, loaded dinner table, where the "two opinionated old Scotch-men" were wont to have their lively talkfests, "exploding their theories, sometimes in cordial agreement, sometimes in heated argument," she offers us this passage:

> Mr. Muir, naturally gentle, kindly, and unobtrusive, ex-pressed, but definitely, his [disbelief] in Dr. Murray's the-ory of geological evolution. Dr. Murray's voice rose in a roar of disputation, banging his fist on the table until the dishes rattled.

> "Rocks are rocks—no matter how they evolved," said Muir, cutting short the debate with a stroke of logic.

> Murray, by all accounts, was a man more likable at a dis-tance than close up, with nobody able to speak in full voice against his tiresome theories. His overbearing presence was as hard to abide as the cockroaches in his kitchen, troops of them, "big black ones, on the sink, others crawling up through the cracks in the old floor boards." What a way to run a hotel! You want to throw up your hands and go home. Fortunately there was always something around that tempted you to stay. For the Muirs it was Andreas Canyon. Off they went with their bedrolls and grub box, Ms. Gaut at their heels, a fresh notebook handy for planned and unplanned need.

What a paradise! The canyon had Muir in raptures: the tall walls and waterfalls, the kaleidoscopic confusion of colors, the jumbled boulders gleaming like polished brass. Six days passed in which interesting plants were found, rock art was viewed, and sentimental songs with many choruses were sung around a campfire, the human voices raised against the night noises, the whisper of wings, the sharp bark of a fox—Ms. Gaut storing up the details as she bites the end of her pen. Best of all, an ailing daughter was made well again, thus bringing Muir's visit to a successful end.

But back to McCallum and his colony to be—Palm Valley it was now grandly called. He had a water supply, a general store, a post office, and a hotel. He was on a roll, burning up body and soul with plans: The McCallum Land Auction Show. The clever man had worked it all out. He had seen to the distribution of flyers—Palm Valley, the Land of Purple Night and Golden Morning . . . Earliest Fruit Region in the State . . . Perpetual Water Rights. He had arranged for a special Southern Pacific excursion train to conduct the speculative hordes to the site. Done and done. Except that a misunderstanding on the part of railroad employees had the train leaving Los Angeles ahead of the advertised time. Hence the attendance from there was regrettably small. But this was a minor matter.

McCallum just didn't know when to quit! Had you descended from the train that auction day, first thing you would have noticed was his promotional stunt: the Indian Willie Marcus tricked out in Arabian robes, a heap of cloth piled on his head. Having thus been reduced, in the space of one event, to the level of sideshow freak at a circus, Marcus was trying his cheerful best to give the Seven Palms station a weird and faraway association with the Promised Land. The camel he was perched upon in no way went unnoticed. In all his life, Marcus had probably never seen such a creature, let alone ridden one. Yet there it was beneath him, big boned and firmly humped, smelly and treacherously alive—although like the robes and turban, it had seen better days.

I think I know where that camel came from. The story begins with a long voyage aboard an odd Noah's Ark, in which several dozens of the one-humped creatures were shipped from Asia Minor to Texas. From there they were led overland to Fort Tejon, home of the army's first and last camel corps. When I read this I wasn't exactly sure where Fort Tejon was; so I looked it up on a Southern California map. It shows up as a black historical site/museum symbol in Kern County, just off I-5 between Lebec and Grapevine.

At Fort Tejon the camels got off to a good start. During field trials they were found to be extremely hardy. They were comfortable in searing heat and freezing cold. They could travel for days without water. They could go for weeks—a lifetime, if need be—browsing on creosote bushes, while mules and horses died of starvation. But positive aspects aside, camels had certain habits that endeared them to no one. They spit prodigiously. They sneezed and vomited in remarkable volume. They roared with indignation while being loaded, snarled and snapped when anyone tried to mount. Even without provocation they were liable to attack, and they always went for the belly. In short, camels were a failure. There was nothing to do but expel them from Fort Tejon. Beyond that, they were sold to circuses, some of them. The rest were simply set adrift in the desert to shift for themselves. Here, for the better part of five decades, they lived in freedom and against considerable odds, prehistoric-looking beasts with undernourished humps.

Back to Willie Marcus then, an Indian on camelback, a single new creature. Having looked him over, head to hoof, the excursionists took their places among the waiting carriages and set off across the dunes for Murray's hotel. Two hours later there they were, spilling from the carriages, ensconcing themselves comfortably in the wrong rooms, stumbling over each other's baggage, sending Murray here and there on senseless errands, and creating all kinds of horrible confusion for his wife. The next morning, fortified by a night's rest, they set off at a smart trot to find their own special place in the sun, the subdivision flags flapping in the breeze, the stakes marking off lots and blocks and fields Ripe with Golden Opportunity.

At last they assembled for the auction—no ordinary auction this, for McCallum had spared no expense. Beef sizzled on the grill. Refreshment tables stood covered with barrels of beer, whiskey, and wine, as free as the air and quite stimulating when the bidding began. A brass band kicked things off, lending a sense of significance to the occasion. Then several speakers, retreating behind a sandstorm of circumlocution, made presentations to which (I trust) everyone listened with an open mind. Everyone wanted to see Palm Valley work. This was no time for skeptics, for the alleged experts who predicted that the hot blasts of mid-summer would "wither" the citrus seedlings and the Whitewater River would "disdain to flow" through McCallum's ditch, at least as far as Palm Valley.

When they ran out of speakers, the auctioneer himself appeared in white gloves, high silk hat, and cutaway coat. Here was a man who knew how to handle a crowd, how to manipulate a bid: "What am I offered, ladies and gentlemen? Who'll give me one hundred dollars, eighty dollars, eighty dollars, fifty-fifty-fifty. Going, going . . . gone! One-third cash, balance in twelve months." Indeed, McCallum could hardly have hoped for a better man or a more receptive crowd. Fifty thousand dollars, right out of the blue, a lush profit in those days. Well, he deserved it. He had thought of everything.

Among the successful bidders was a Mr. L. M. Holt, owner of the *Riverside Press and Horticulturist*, from whence came, in the following months, glowing progress reports: Judge McCallum's pea patch was "ready for picking." Superintendent Bordwell's orange grove was "looking well." Reverend Norris's melon patch was "looking finely . . . so, dear Western friends, look out for carloads of melons from Palm Valley a month earlier than from elsewhere." For all the earlier skepticism, when the hot blasts of mid-summer came, the citrus seedlings still took "a cheerful view of life" and went on "sprouting and putting on new garments." As for the Whitewater River, "each day and all night long it comes to us in so great volume that a part of it has to be diverted from the canal and allowed to waste its wetness on the desert sand."

So far so good for Judge, Rancher, Developer McCallum. But things were not going as well for Indian Agent McCallum. Several years back he had resigned his post amid accusations that he had taken improper title to tribally-owned Tahquitz Canyon. Now he was being accused of "playing a secondary permissive role" when Welwood Murray diverted the tribe's hot spring for the pleasure of his hotel guests. Additionally, both men stood accused of "getting up a scheme" whereby they paid the Indians "a trifle" for title to land surrounding the tribal cemetery. To make matters worse, they then denied the Indians access to their ancestral graves. A new cemetery site was chosen, but apparently McCallum interfered with the reburial, because charges were made that bodies "were being plowed up left and right." Finally, both men were accused and tried in the United States District Court for "felonious removal of wood" from tribal land. The suit dragged on for four years, and ultimately both men were acquitted, which doesn't mean they were found innocent.

The court trial was one thing. The Big Drought was quite another. As predicted the Whitewater River disdained to flow through McCallum's ditch, which of course made the value of expert opinion abundantly clear. As for the value of water rights, the method of the day was to get water any way you could. So there were more accusations—the details are vague—and again the Indian agent was brought down from Banning, and again he settled things in favor of the Indians. But old habits die hard, and Welwood Murray continued to divert the forbidden Tahquitz Creek, already enfeebled by the drought, to his precious trees. Perhaps to get into the mood of this, you need to see the old man, now nearing eighty and apparently close to dementia, his beard wild, his skullcap askew, his ridiculous frock coat flapping around his knees, his feet straddling the head gate—a sad old heron standing pointless watch at a pond without fish. On the one hand, the Indians, armed with a decree. On the other hand, Murray, otherwise armed, opening the sluice gate while everyone slept, settling things the traditional way. Again the Indian agent was brought down, and again he settled things in favor of the Indians. But there's no point in continuing a story that has been repeated hundreds of times over across the country. Except to say that it has long been a matter of local discussion whether Murray and McCallum were visionary pioneers or rascally scoundrels who spoiled Indian-Anglo relationships for generations to come. Palm Springs has every right to claim them as founding fathers, and every reason not to.

Little remains to be told. Shut off at last from Tahquitz Creek, his trees dying, one and all, the long-suffering Murray must have felt more than a twinge of irritation at McCallum for dragging him into all this. "We are now feeble, and sometimes very sad," he wrote in a faded hand to his son George. Wishing himself out of the entire business, he sold the hotel to Cornelia and Florilla White, who had by the greatest of good fortune just entered the village from Mexico. Then he left Palm Springs to resume his retirement in Banning, where I'm sure the Indians thought he properly belonged. From there, he passed peacefully to the land of white robes and golden harps, leaving his name attached to the canyon as a reminder of what, I imagine, no Indian wanted to remember.

Years before this, McCallum himself had passed into history. As he faced his final verdict, he could only look back on the ruin his life had become, this man who had achieved such success through force of character and seizure of opportunity. His agrarian dream, which had been going so well, was as dead as his orchard. His water company was in virtual bankruptcy, its irrigation ditches untended, its wooden trestles collapsed. To make his life even more tragic, fate had carried off his innocent children, one by one: Johnnie, at the age of twenty-six, dead of tuberculosis; Harry dead at age thirty of tuberculosis; Wallace dead at age twenty-nine of heart disease complicated by alcoholism; May dead at age forty-five of complications from typhoid. All of them gone to their graves (only Pearl lived on to restore his fortunes, but this was in the future and he would never know). Such reflections weakened

McCallum spiritually as old age weakened him physically. I imagine that his heart failed him in more ways than one.

* * *

If you are hiking north from Murray Canyon, you will come to Andreas Canyon, where so much in the way of variety is going on. The prime elements are rocks, beautiful, blocky rocks, bright in their quartzes and colorful in their lichens; they are like houses standing in the sand, with rock wrens on their roofs. Here, between high-walled outcroppings, lies a creepered world of endless shade, a fantasy of palms, cottonwoods, sycamores, and birches—big trees with tangles of grapevines winding up their trunks, using the trunks for trellises. This is as close as some of us desert rats have ever come to a real jungle, and we have only to wait a few minutes to see half a dozen luminous green parrots come screaming out of the canopy. After languishing behind brass bars for who knows how many years, they have somehow found each other and adapted to life in the palms.

Andreas Canyon was named after the Cahuilla Indian John Andreas, who, in modern fashion, was called captain instead of chief. Had you been here in the latter part of the nineteenth century, you would have found Andreas beating out an austere existence for himself half a mile up his namesake canyon, on a fertile bench "picturesque in the extreme," if a visiting San Francisco journalist was qualified to judge.

The wild vines make fantastic curtains of greenery, and so closely are their limbs mattered together that in summer there seems to be a broad, thick swaying wall of dense leafage encircling the many cup-like pools in the glistening white rocks. Andreas here laid out a vineyard and cultivated peach trees, but against the peach he one day took a grudge and chopped them down, for, said he: "The birds come here and nest and tell one to another that soon the grapes will be ripe, and they come and eat them."

Captain Andreas was a hard-working man who had been taught by unscrupulous whites how best to use his vineyard. His operation was simple. First he crushed the harvested grapes beneath his feet. Then he fermented the grape juice and distilled it in something that might have come straight out of the Kentucky hills. Then he dripped the firewater into old champagne bottles that quickly found their way to his tribe, these people who had small physical and less moral resistance to alcohol. Andreas well knew that consumption of alcohol by Indians, if not the manufacture, was forbidden by law. He also knew that the laws of the land do not fully operate in tribal territory, as we all have been made rather tiresomely aware lately. So it was up to Welwood Murray—of all people—to dispense justice. Although Murray was remarkably flexible when it came to encroaching on tribal water rights, he was entirely rigid when it came to this shiftless Andreas corrupting the tribal labor force that so willingly performed the back-breaking work Murray disliked doing for himself. Against such a man Andreas had no hope. How dearly I would have loved to witness, from a safe distance, what followed: Murray, red-faced and short of breath, flourishing his fists at Andreas, defying him to the teeth as a villain, as a traitor to his people, driving him insane in that typical Murray way, the hell-fire speech framed to the point of memorization, the exact words of which, alas, are lost to history. Then jacking himself up to a battering climax, with a few well-placed kicks, Murray sent the hillbilly still sprawling, and with it, the last of the vintage. Thus the storm blew over without further injury.

* * *

North of Andreas Canyon lies the canyon called Tahquitz, as conspicuous for its famous waterfall as for its sorry history of abuse. In 1937 the canyon served as Shangri-la for Frank Capra's *Lost Horizon*, and nothing good has happened there ever since. Old folks, and some not that old, remember Easter week in the 1960s and what went on up there among the creosote bushes and tumble-down boulders: all those college kids, full of pagan enthusiasm, injecting, smoking, guzzling just about anything they could get their hands on, with not even so much as a string of love beads between themselves and the sun. "Hot-Blooded Youth on the Loose," the *Desert Sun* always gave it full treatment.

Especially unfavorable press was given to the Easter week of 1969, the news of which reached me in Los Angeles. As a former flower child who had only recently wilted back into straight society, I read with interest accounts of an invasion the *Sun* had no intention of hiding on its society page. That year the Pacific beaches were closed, polluted with oil in the north and raw sewage in the south. So word went out: the scene was Palm Springs. And since there was never much for the kids to do, beyond the primitive delights of Tahquitz Canyon, the city had approved two rock concerts. Canned Heat, Black Pearl, Moby Grape, Ike and Tina Turner—everybody would be there.

The week started out like any normal Easter week, and the

merchants, having tidied up their restaurants and shops, were looking forward to the surge in business. But it quickly became clear that things would be anything but normal. The crowds were bigger, younger, wilder, and not so incidentally, drunker.

Then the first rock concert at the Palm Springs Drive-In, and a crush of fans, opting not to pay admission, stormed unmolested through the gates. No sooner had the press sent out that story ("What a Riot"), then the second concert, this one at Angels Stadium, brought a fresh debacle. This time the concert-goers came up against a helmeted force, batons at the ready. Bottles flew. Plumes of tear gas were fired back. But repression, as usual, only made matters worse. The mob, now hell-bent on mayhem, crossed the street and began tearing apart a strip mall. Harlan Moore's service station came next— a crash of plate glass. Moore snapped a clip into his gun, fired into the mob, and wounded three kids, one of whom spent the holy days hospitalized with a bullet lodged near his heart.

The city declared a state of emergency. Roadblocks went up and all incoming youths were turned away from the shutdown city. What the kids understood even more clearly was how much they had outraged the Indians, who would no longer look with indifference, much less with favor, on camping in Tahquitz Canyon. With that, a hundred deputies charged into the highest reaches and frog-marched the kids into the center of the city, where there was little chance they would find hotel accommodations. It was crazy. It was shocking, all that litter they left behind, the middens of beer cans, wine bottles, discarded tents and bathing suits. Even more shocking was the graffiti, a slogan on every rock, Jesus Saves on one entire wall.

Banning rock concerts and closing Tahquitz Canyon to the public for the next thirty years didn't end the Easter week tradition, although things tapered off in the seventies as doomed youth was dragged kicking and screaming toward its inescapable fate as responsible adult. But with the early eighties came the unrestrained spirit of self-indulgence seen in previous years. Spring Break it was now called to remove any semblance of holiness. Those kids, how they did love to party! From dusk to dawn, they cruised Palm Canyon Drive bumper-to-bumper, hooting, whistling, burning rubber in their muscle cars, popping wheelies on their Harleys, their babes in thong bikinis hanging on to their backs (*Playboy* was there to shoot one of its pictorials). They mooned the foolhardy sightseers, yanked off their bikini tops, soaked them with balloons and squirt guns filled with ink, dye, *urine.* Again the media flashed headlines across the nation: "Palm Springs Rampage." "Youths Run Amok." "Holiday Youths Run Wild."

Here was the problem as newly-elected mayor Sonny Bono saw it. Over the years the city's indulgence had put the city in a fix, really a succession of fixes. It was about time for council members to come to their collective senses. And that they did, with a flurry of new laws forbidding water balloons, squirt guns, thong bikinis, mooning, and sidewalk boozing. Cruising was forbidden; a maze of concrete barriers made cruising all but impossible. That dude Bono, he didn't know what he was doing, or he knew what he was doing and didn't give a damn. For fifty years cruising Palm Canyon Drive had been the lifeblood of Easter week, a reminder, as if I needed any, of my own teenage days of yore. Then, as if to add insult to injury, youths were invited to view wildflowers, play golf-croquet, tour recycling and composting exhibits—the city had sifted through all kinds of ideas and come up with something called the Harvest Festival. There it was, the last straw. "They've gone overboard, man. We won't be back next year. We'll go where we're wanted."

Highly anticlimactic it might seem, but that's the way it was, and that's the way it is today. Lake Havasu City, they're all yours.

* * *

North of Tahquitz lies the canyon called Tachevah, which means, if you get it right, plain view. I like the Cahuilla tradition of naming a place by those words that simply describe it. So it is *Cawish wa-wat-acha*, mighty mountain; *E va we*, wind blows all the time; *Hunwit hekik*, place of the bear; *Gash mo*, crunching of sand as one walks. And what happened here at *You koo hal ya me*? you ask, place of many brains. It's more commonly called Bullseye Rock, just as curious a name. I've seen the rock; it's a polished block of granite that rises shear above the sand like a profound geological statement. I've climbed it, hauled myself up using only the faintest finger-grips, my brother in the lead, calling down to me as the distance between us grew. Although the scene at the top added yet another dimension of significance—and a sensation that words cannot approach—without the history it's an empty name. I went to the library for details.

According to Cahuilla historians, peace, along with a sense of commitment, was built into the aboriginal system, not only through marriages, but through songs, ideas, rituals, and above all, a sophisticated trade in such diversified items as beads, shells, obsidian, salt, fish, pinyon nuts . . . the list is engagingly long. Certainly there were conflicts, occasionally. But they resulted in a single encounter, and loss of life was minimal. Complete annihilation of an enemy was unknown. Except, as far as I can tell, at Seven Palms.

What went on over there at Seven Palms, in those other, darker days before the railroad came through, were conflicting claims to the wild wheat harvest. Sooner or later things were bound to get ugly. With numbers on their side, the Palm Springs Indians decided a war was in order, even though there weren't many Indians to make war on at Seven Palms. Bows and arrows were assembled, a strategy was devised, and the entire tribe at Seven Palms, caught off guard one morning, came to a sticky end. The battlefield, red with valiant blood, was made even redder when the fallen warriors were beheaded. Then, with little consideration given to distance, the heads were carried home, dripping, to Palm Canyon, dashed against Bullseye Rock, and deprived of their brains—a custom, I imagine, mired in layers of meaning.

I'd like to believe that Tachevah Canyon has such a rousing past, but even that invaluable storyteller Patencio seems stumped: "There is no story," we hear him say. Even more discouraging is the canyon's future and the future of its resident bighorn sheep. I am particularly nervous about a project called the Preserve at Mountain Falls: time-share villas, clubhouse, artificial lake, golf course—quite the deal. *Preserve*? Surely a contradiction. Mountain *Falls*? Surely a joke. Mineral stains left by a rivulet of moisture have created the illusion of a waterfall, but Dry Falls is dry in fact, as well as in name.

Community television keeps us abreast of such projects, making our beleaguered bureaucrats among the most scrutable and obvious in the country. As a rule, following the opening prayer for guidance, city council sessions begin around dinnertime and rarely finish before ten o'clock (and some of the hours between can drag heavily when you don't understand the technical language). Nevertheless, the impending Mountain Falls decision drew a vibrant audience that filled the council chamber to its remotest corners. On a businesslike platform above the throng, Mayor Will Kleindienst, always articulate, composed, and good at fending off antagonisms his predecessors have incurred, presided over the four-member council, everyone seated in chairs exceedingly well adapted for lengthy hearings. The pro-and-anti format was familiar, with the audience being forced to choose sides, each side working with a harmony of wills toward what each perceived as a good end. During seven hours of testimony, men in dark suits came forth to the microphone, spread their speeches upon the rostrum, and in conspiratorial tones presented the proposal in the best possible light. Then, hauling out the Endangered Species Act, the opposition came forth and presented the proposal otherwise. "There are twenty-five Peninsular bighorn sheep struggling to survive in the San Jacinto Mountains," Wayne Brechtel from the Sierra Club pointed out to the council. "You have the authority to deny the project." Homeowner Larry Liguori took the floor and put it another way: "I'm telling you this is no place for a golf course," to which a good portion of the room responded with hand clapping and spirited shouts. Considering that Tachevah Canyon defines the fashionable Las Palmas neighborhood, no one was surprised to see that Liguori's neighbors had come out from behind their high walls to stop the city from spoiling their solitude.

The fact that most people in attendance that night expressed contempt for the project would seem to make it moot—except that everyone sensed it was not. As a result, there were so many speakers, all running to the end of their allotted three minutes, that by ten o'clock what they had to say was less important than how long they took to say it. At the weary stroke of midnight, the mere thought of more talk led the mayor to announce, with sincere regret, that he had done his mayoral duty and was going home to bed. Braving a roomful of frowns, he passed the gavel to the mayor pro tem, apologized to the crowd, and sought his pillow, after which the debate lumbered on for close to three more hours. While the mayor slept, the last motion was put before the council, seconded, and carried by a three-one vote. The time for talk had ended; it was time to move dirt. Tachevah Canyon, up to now unprofitably occupied by bighorn sheep, would become a golf course—would that be number ninety-eight for the Coachella Valley? or number ninety-nine? That is, of course, if the project survives litigation.

* * *

North of Tachevah lies the canyon called Chino, the last in this series. It also is about to join modern times. Here at the foot of the steepest rock face in the country, the proposed Shadowrock Resort threatens the sheep with yet another golf course. But perhaps the city can't resist adding one or two more, making it an even hundred.

To drive up Chino Canyon is to go back through the un-written stories of the Palm Springs Indians, through a timeless rhythm of aboriginal existence. Envision if you will the groves of slender sycamores; the springs bubbling up through the sand, hot for bathing, cool for drinking; the patchwork of veg-etable gardens irrigated by stone-lined ditches; the thatched huts that seem to rise out of the gardens themselves. And yet even in Eden nature can be hideous, as witnessed by the boy Francisco Patencio:

> The people had their things all packed up to come down into the valley below; the garden was all gathered together, the corn was stacked in piles, everything they had planted was stacked for carrying away. Then my people saw a great white cloud rising over San Jacinto mountain. It was coming very fast . . . the thunder and lightning began coming, then rain and wind. Such a storm was not remembered among the Indians. The floods began roaring down. My people only had time to catch up their children and rush up the mountain side to save their lives.

What Patencio describes is an appalling exhibition of the earth's power to destroy itself without any assistance from human engineering. The flood mobilized everything that lay before it, every last bit and piece of Patencio's childhood, driven asunder, washed over, flushed away.

> The homes of my people and all they had were gone for ever. All the harvest they had raised was gone, and all the good land, it was gone, too. Where the grass was green for animals, and the soil good to raise things to eat for the people, there were only piles of great rocks and wash-out gorges. My people never tried to raise anything there any more.

That would seem to end the story, but Patencio adds a post-script, this final insult:

> An Indian from one of the tribes in the valley below was coming to visit the Palm Springs Indians. At a place a few

miles west of Indian Wells he could not believe what he saw with his eyes. There was a wild harvest of corn, pumpkins, and many other things, lying ready for the taking. He turned back and brought his people, who carried home all that they had found.

* * *

Having gotten a late start today, I will hike no more than a few miles up Palm Canyon—not that I have promises to keep or anything you could call real work waiting at home. But the Indians think I'm on a schedule, and if I'm not back at Hermits Bench by sunset it is assumed by those in charge that I have become lost or injured. Chances are excellent that an embarrassing rescue will be launched on my behalf, whether I need rescuing or not.

Everywhere the topography is irregular and varied. Contorted side canyons breach the hillsides, their entrances guarded by miserable thickets of mesquite. Even nastier than mesquite, if such can be imagined, is catsclaw acacia, an "affectionate creature," to quote Smeaton Chase, "that grapples you to its soul with hooks of steel and loves to keep you there, taking a double hold for every claw you gently disengage. You will not go far on the desert without meeting the cat-claw, nor will you part without cursing it."

Music comes from everywhere: creeksong, frogsong, birdsong. Every bush seems to hold a small energetic wren in full throat. I hear a Bewick's wren, loud and bubbling; a rock wren's varied trills; a cactus wren's unmusical, low-pitched cackle; a canyon wren's long descending whistle, remarkably like the voice of the creek itself. Above me a hawk cries out, a red-tailed I see when I look, swinging in lazy circles on a wind I cannot feel. A flash of black and orange proves to be, on second glance—and with plumage this brilliant there is always a second glance—three hooded orioles giving chase. Butterflies float by, scraps of pure color: a monarch, a swallowtail, a checkerspot, a metalmark, a dozen painted ladies flying in fits and starts . . . *two* dozen more. I put it all in my notebook.

* * *

In fits and starts my mind returns to a scene that has nothing to do with butterflies. It is 1938, and for weeks the village press has devoted their front pages to Palm Canyon, the Movie:

> A lush tropical jungle blossoms today in the heart of the desert, where skilled nurserymen have performed a botanical miracle by the transplanting of $20,000 worth of rare tropical plants and trees. Seven miles south of Palm Springs, this fortune in foliage surrounds a crystal lagoon in Palm Canyon, where the be-saronged Dorothy Lamour and Ray Milland are engaged in making Paramount's "Her Jungle Love," first jungle picture ever filmed in Technicolor.

There is no overt connection between a desert canyon and a classic jungle, but Hollywood has blurred our sense of other places as well. Creating a crystal lagoon and a "realistic" cave where none existed called for exorbitant fakery. It called for a system of cables extending half a mile up the canyon, along which husky "Paramounters" pushed dolly carts loaded with lumber, plaster, and gypsum. Up the canyon, they sent papier-mâché palm trees, twenty of them, never mind that twenty-five *hundred* palm trees were already growing in the canyon, they weren't growing in exactly the right spot. The fake palms weren't so much planted as posed in front of the fake cliffs and the fake rocks that had been hoisted in for basically the same reason.

After weeks of work, the canyon became what the press was pleased to call "superbly realistic and scientifically charming." To the huge discomfort of a colony of ground squirrels who had come to look upon the canyon as their own, the creek had been dammed to form a crystal lagoon topped with floating islands of flowering plants. Not only were these tender exotics many, they were unaccustomed to the water in the lagoon. So harsh with alkali was this water, the plants fell sick with the "equivalent of acute nausea." At which point, the skilled nurserymen were called back to replant, providing more fodder for the press.

If Academy Awards were given for sheer bloody-minded persistence, *Her Jungle Love* would have made a grand sweep. To give the fake scenery a livelier atmosphere, to make it look more like the India called for in the script, a mad assemblage of animals had been hoisted to the set, the colorful cranes and playful tiger cubs creating some strange reality games of their own. How Jiggs the Ape arrived wasn't reported, only that he was big and ugly, with a "rosy and hairless bottom" that proved too brilliant for Technicolor and had to be "dumbed down" by Max Factor to avoid offending the delicate sensibilities of the movie-goers.

Everyone got a jolt the morning an unscripted deer, understandably confused (Who put that lagoon there? Where did that cave come from?), charged through the set, leaving havoc in its wake. The press, unable to resist any of it, reported it all.

At the same time, the tourists came like they had never come before, a great goggling crowd more attracted to the jungle made by Hollywood than the canyon made by nature. For six weeks the film crew struggled to keep them out of the shots.

The film's title betrays the primitive nature of the narrative. To cut a dumb script short, during a violent storm, Hero Miland crashes his silver monoplane on an uncharted island. Then, with a survivor's elation, he teaches love to a woman raised by wild animals: Jungle Princess Lamour of the clinging sarong.

A typhoon opened the picture—Special Effects at work, the huge wind machines operating full blast, supplemented by an elaborate drip-drizzle-deluge pumping system, everything hoisted in by the makeshift tram. After spending so much time setting up the scene, the moment arrived to shoot it. Lights! Palm trees! Action! The wind machines whipped the canyon to a tropical lather, and the crew got some splendid takes. But no sooner had they finished patting themselves on the back, then "God's own wind" blew through the set, creating such havoc among the tender exotics, the nurserymen had to be called back again to replant, during which time, you can bet, the idled cast went on a bender.

Filming resumed, keeping the press active and alert:

Dorothy Lamour, star of the picture, was supposed to hurl a knife into the trunk of a tree, beside which, all unsuspecting, stood the hero of the jungle thriller, Ray Milland. Miss Lamour, who is an accomplished knife thrower, had practiced the scene several times each time with a dummy taking the place of hero Milland. When the scene rehearsed to his satisfaction, the director,

George Archainbaud, called for the take, and as the scene was to be a close up took his position near the tree. When the cameras started grinding Miss Lamour drew back her arm to hurl the knife, but her foot slipped and the knife went wild, missing hero and tree, but grazing the arm of Director Archianbaud.

Somewhat white about the gills, having just come within inches of sudden death, Archainbaud, blood streaming from his wounded arm, was one of the few to keep his head in the general excitement that followed. Actor Milland, the color slowly returning under his make-up, expressed a willingness to try the scene again, but Miss Lamour, who up to that point in her career had avoided murdering anybody, "appeared on the verge of a nervous collapse and production was ordered stopped for the day."

It's hard to say when Palm Canyon, the Movie passed out of existence. "Number of Visitors Sets Record in Canyon" was a headline one morning, the reporters beside themselves with enthusiasm. Weeks later, "Jiggs Has Birthday in Canyon" was only a short column buried on the society page, one dull word following another. Then, as if on cue, the press took no more notice. Barring stills and an extra take or two, the film had been declared finished, and the cast, having wrapped their roles, moved on to other sets of unreality. At some point, the husky Paramounters dismantled the plaster facades, the wind blew the last props across the sand, and the alkali killed off the exotic flora. As for the movie itself, I wish I could report that it had an everlasting effect on the course of movie-making. But it didn't. As it turns out, *Her Jungle Love* no longer exists in archive or rerun because the film, based on cellulose nitrate, was intensely flammable and prone to turn into chemical mush if improperly stored. But on balance, who cares. Images of canyon-as-jungle shouldn't be preserved in any form.

* * *

To emerge from the Jungle Love palms is to shift from the vertical to the horizontal, from the intimate to the expansive, from the shadows to the dazzling sunlight. Here the trail is less trampled, the loneliness lovelier, and the prospect of encountering a rattlesnake more likely at every step—which is good if you like a little action on your hikes. Just listen and your ears will tell you when something mighty scary is about to happen. At first you don't recognize it for what it is, not so much a rattle as a furious *ts-ts-ts-ts*. Then suddenly you see it, coiled on a sunny ledge, its scaly hide the color and texture of granite, its forked tongue licking the air . . . although how, in the midst of your terror, are you expected to jot down such details. Big snake, is what you think. Lots of venom. Slowly you back away and make for safety, each step sending the snake into a new spasm of buzzing. Now your eyes are opened wider than before, and every twitch of bush, every crackle of twig has an ominous meaning of its own.

This upper part of Palm Canyon is not beautiful in the pastoral sense, the green sense. In the broiling heat of August you wouldn't think it was worth much, this graveyard of plants, the life burned out of them. Nothing stirs. The ground squirrels refuse to come out of their cool hidey holes. The blackthroated sparrows, unwilling or unable to fly, retire to the hypothetical shade of the mesquite, where they pant through parted beaks and hope for better times. There are no quail in the washes, no rabbits in the brush, and what the coyotes live on, unless on one another, is a mystery. Crowds, needless to say, are not a concern.

Smoke completes the utter misery when brushfires break out in the chaparral country on the west side of the San Jacintos. Like a thunderhead the smoke rises above the ridge, turning the sun from burnt white to blood red. All it takes is the careless or deliberate touch of a match. The wind does the rest, turning the flicker into a fire, an explosion of flame.

Damn the summer, bless the spring. April on an El Nino year ridicules the austerity of August. The hillsides are covered with alien grasses, so tall and lush I wouldn't be surprised to see a flock of white woolly lambs come gamboling around the corner. Telephone hotlines and Web sites have sprung up as fast as the flowers. By early afternoon, the entire vacationing public will be arriving at Hermits Bench to celebrate. You can tell what's going on by the number of out-of-state plates. They're out from the Keystone State, the Green Mountain State, the Last Frontier, the Land of Lincoln . . .

So many flowers, so many armyworms—creatures we have met earlier. There's something almost fateful about the way in which, once you are thoroughly hooked into a subject, odd bits of information keep gravitating your way. Which brings me to a circled item in my notes. Although at this stage it seems merely showy to report it, nevertheless I shall, now that I have grown sufficiently fond of armyworms.

In 1884, my notes read, William Greenwood Wright witnessed a remarkable event near Araby Point, directly below Bob Hope's house on the hill. *Pe ya hot mor am muh* the Cahuillas called it, place of the armyworms. Here is Wright preserving it for posterity in an issue of the *Overland Monthly*:

In an hour we came to the caterpillar pasture. The sand is dotted with mats and patches of a procumbent plant, much resembling in flower the common sand verbena, *abronia*, on which vast armies of caterpillars are feeding; they are huge worms three and four inches long. Another small army of Indians . . . are out gathering them as though they were huckleberries, for use as food.

And again:

Seizing a fat worm, they pull off its head, and by a dexterous jerk the viscera are ejected, and the wriggling carcass is put into a small basket, or strung in strings upon the arm or about the neck, till occasion is found to put them into a large receptacle. At night, these Indians carry their prey home, where they have a great feast. Indians from a long distance came to these worm feasts, and it is a time of great rejoicing among them. The larvae that are not consumed at the time (and they eat incredible quantities), are put upon ground previously heated by a fire, and thoroughly dried; [then] they are packed away whole, or pulverized into a meal.

As to what armyworms taste like, let's just say "not good" and leave it at that. As an armyworm connoisseur, I am hopeless. Happy and hungry, but hopeless.

I see that El Nino has resurrected a bewildering display of perennials in Palm Canyon. Equally splendid are the small annuals that quickly rush from seed to seed—ephemerals is a better word, they're so soft and succulent, and in some years, nonexistent. Desert stars bloom cheek-to-cheek at my toes, forming a carpet that is heartless to tread upon. Orange poppies and creamy blazing stars bloom at my ankles, violet phacelia and yellow rock-peas at my knees; and at my waist, shrubby members of the mallow family, firmly dedicated to rosiness. There are less conspicuous flowers that a trained mind could name. Mine is not trained. I carry guidebooks around to help me recognize the flowers, and I am continually disappointed in myself for not remembering all their names. I do know the prickly poppy, the "fried egg flower" suggesting sunny side up; and the loco weed that "locoed" the old cowboys' horses, "dispossessed them of self-control and made them subject to fits of ungovernable action." I can tell you a good deal about datura, that sinister shrub from the nightshade family, known variously as sacred datura, Don Juan's datura, devil's trumpet, mad apple, moon lily, and dream weed. To the botanist it's *Datura meteloides, Datura inoxia, Datura discolor* . . . at least fifty species occur throughout the world. It's the Spaniard's *belladonna de pobre*, poor man's belladonna. It's the Mexican's *torna-loco*, becoming crazy. It's *toloache* to the Cahuillas. It's thornapple. It's jimsonweed, a corruption of Jamestown weed, after Jamestown, Virginia. And therein lies an old story.

In 1676, in an effort to quell a tobacco tax rebellion, British troops landed at the Jamestown colony. One evening, in an effort to prevent scurvy, the regimental cooks went forth into the wasteland of weeds and collected ingredients for a dinner salad, possibly purslane, probably dandelion greens, and certainly the local *Datura stramonium*. Some of the men, observed Robert Beverly, ate plentifully,

> the effect of which was a very pleasant comedy, for they
> turned natural fools . . . One would blow up a feather in
> the air; another would dart straws at it with much fury;

and another, stark naked, was sitting up in a corner like a monkey, grinning; a fourth would fondly kiss and paw his companions . . . Indeed they were not very cleanly; for they would have wallowed in their own excrement, if they had not been prevented.

My approach to intriguing subjects like this has always been to sit down at the keyboard and fire up the Internet. My search is often hit-and-miss, but with a little luck gradually I begin to learn what I want to know (and all manner of what I don't want to know). Thus I typed in *datura* more times than I care to remember, and I found hundreds of Web sites, with ads flashing and wiggling across the margins. My eyes flicked past datura history, datura botany, datura chemistry. Past disclaimers and warnings. Past hospital records and first-person accounts of extreme suffering: hallucinations, delirium, convulsions, stupor, coma . . . Past recipes: grind it at full moon, mix it with ethanol, stir it into warm Vaseline, and rub it on skin. But do not eat it. Do not explore this one, Dude!! Two exclamation marks, and no wonder. In the simplest terms, if you are looking for one of the most potent plant hallucinogens known to science, look no further than datura. But then, I'm only giving the facts as I know them. Don't call me, Dude. Consult the Web.

Another exclamation mark, at least implicit, for what I learned about the "Datura Junkie Moth," aka the sphinx moth, aka the armyworm—a creature I have already explored in these pages perhaps too much at length. And yet the topic taunts. You see, unlike most moths, the sphinx has evolved mouthparts that fit nicely into the long slender nectar canals of the datura blossoms. Stranger yet, the chemistry of the nectar may have evolved to ensure repeated visits by the moth through the medium of drug addiction. This would explain why scientists have observed the moths hovering over the plants, waiting to catch the long, pleated buds in the act of un-furling—at which point they hit the flowers, crawl into the corolla throat, and suck up the nectar, their little tails cocked with pleasure. Then away they go, their consciousness altered, their flight erratic, their landings clumsy. Oddly enough, the moths seem to like being intoxicated: they always come back for more.

Moving upcanyon, I see that times are flush for other in-sects as well. A bevy of bees works the blossoms of the desert apricot, from which they'll make their crop of honey, sweetest stuff the aboriginal Indians ever tasted. Where encelia bushes dominate the landscape, big black and orange meloid beetles feed on the daisy-like flowers, pairs of beetles coupled end-to-end, feeding and mating at the same time. It's not a good idea to annoy them right now; their bright color advertises their poison.

Where there are flowers, there are insects eating those flow-ers, and lizards eating those insects, and lizards eating those lizards, swallowing them whole and alive. A zebra-tail lizard dashes about on some important errand, tail held high above his head. Catching sight of me, he stops dead and pretends not to be there. On a rock, orange with lichen, a side-blotched lizard basks in the dependable sunshine. He turns his startled face in my direction—"a bony little goblin," to borrow again from the admirable Chase, "with a leer in the eye that comes close to being devilish."

The horned lizards live here, horny toads we called them as kids, referring to the armature of horny spines on their heads.

Their backs are bumpy, their legs short and bowed. They can change color to match their surroundings and thus are invisible to the untrained eye. In frustration I have stood looking at a spot I have looked at three times before, while someone shouted, "It's there in the sand, see it? There! Right there! Can't you see it? Oh, darn, now it's gone."

Here is a lizard whose great size makes him easy to spot, and I like him for that very reason. There he sits, fixing me with his eyes, a prehistoric strangeness among the rocks. He doesn't look exactly like the poisonous gila monster, but with his chubby legs, potbelly, and baggy, slightly beaded skin, he comes close. In fact, he's a non-poisonous chuckwalla, *Sauromalus obesus* (plump lizard)—Chuck to his friends. Boulder piles offer the warmth he loves and the convenient crevasses he scuttles into for safety. Try to drag him from his refuge and he will gulp in air, blow himself up like a balloon, wedge himself more tightly in place, and with dozy reptilian patience, wait for you to go away.

Upon catching sight of a chuckwalla, the aboriginal Cahuilla would invariably lick his lips and ready his chuckwalla hook. Highly prized were the young chucks; charred over an improvised spit, their flesh was tender and sweet. But watch out for the old ones; they could dull your taste for all lizards for all time. This I can't confirm, and heaven keep me from trying.

The trail continues its upward trend, leaving the creek far below. From perches in the cliff, white-throated swifts careen dramatically, their sharp wings somehow working to keep them airborne. From creek to sky, the cliff is so sheer it could be an overhang; I don't venture close enough to the crumbling brink to find out. As it is, I'm beginning to feel slightly anxious here, with several high-walled arroyos between me and Hermits Bench, and the sky shifting to darker shades of gray, signaling the forecasted storm. When you travel at the base of a mountain, you're apt to come abruptly upon these arroyos, carved almost at a stroke by the flush of water. One cloud can dump a year's worth of rain in a few minutes and woe to anyone in the way.

Wherever the hillsides are rocky, the yucca is in bloom, a creamy-white flame in a candelabra of sharply-pointed leaves. Here, too, grows the agave, awaiting its season of glory. It's a plant of leisurely development, Charles Francis Saunders tells us,

> quite well along in its teens, or possibly out of them, before the supreme effort of its life—its blossoming— occurs. Once it is ripe for this business, it transacts it quickly. A juicy bud, resembling the tip of a huge asparagus sprout, thrusts up its head from the heart of the clustered, dagger-like leaves, and rapidly rises upon a lengthening stalk until at a height of eight or ten feet it breaks into a great, loose shower of small, bell-shaped yellow flowers. This accomplished, the plant shrivels up and dies.

Agave, known variously as mescal and century plant, gave itself wholeheartedly to the Cahuillas; a single plant kept a family in food for days. It could also be stored for long periods of time—months, if not years. Saunders knew all this when, in preparation for his wonderfully titled story "Antonio Bakes Mescal and Tells Somewhat of the Stars," he went "mescaling" with the old Indian gentleman and learned the process "from a to izzard."

Antonio was small and thin-faced, "rather leaden of complexion, and of an aspect totally unlike the average California aboriginal, who is usually heavy to obesity and very dusky." For an Indian, he was talkative, his English "bizarre at best" and seasoned with an "occasional dash of Spanish." The landscape he led Saunders through that early April in 1920 was arid, desolate, and cluttered with "as irritable, prickly, and crabbed a floral brood as you would be likely to find anywhere."

Upon finding a mescal plant in prime condition, Antonio chopped out the bud with an ax and lifted it from its "bristling cradle." (Traditionally, the Indians used a pole made of oak or mountain mahogany, with one end beveled like a chisel.) He sliced off and discarded the tip of the bud, put the butt in a gunnysack, then ransacked the hillsides for a "suitable number." In a sandy hollow, where several fire-blackened stones lay about in a circle, he dropped the sack of mescal butts. He dug out the pit several feet deep, lined the sides and bottom with flat stones, and laid the mescal butts in a circle around the rim. He built a roaring fire in the pit, and when the ashes and embers made a substantial bed, he buried the butts and covered the whole with earth.

"*Bueno*," he observed. "To-morrow when the sun gets there"—pointing to the zenith—"we come again and eat him."

Thirty hours later the steaming pit was as fragrant as a molasses barrel. With the tip of his shovel Antonio tossed the mescal butts out of the ashes.

My heart sank at the sight of the blackened chunks, for they seemed hopelessly overdone—burnt to a crisp, in fact. This, however, proved to be but a surface condition.

Paring away the charred outside of one of the pieces, I found the heart to be a tender, sticky, brownish mass, quite sweet, and of a flavor suggesting warm pineapple [this I can confirm] . . . I doubt if the sackful which Antonio carried back with him to share with his family and *parientes* lasted over one sitting.

Besides agave, Saunders crabbed floral brood certainly suggests cacti in bloom, many of which compete for the photographer's attention. Most striking are the beavertail in brilliant magenta and the hedgehog in purplish red. Most remarkable is the corkseed, small enough to fit nicely into a windowsill flower pot, yet blossoming in a huge way, somehow pushing its rosy petals through the fishhook spines no worse for wear. Most conspicuous is the bisnaga, an upright cylindrical cactus built like a barrel, pleated like an accordion, and crowned with a ring of lemon-yellow flowers. Study the bisnaga long enough and you will come across historical accounts of its use as an emergency water source—a minefield of misleading information that keeps plant authorities in stitches. Drive a pipe into one side of a bisnaga, writes one old enthusiast, build a fire on the other side, and by that you will "secure a slow supply of water straight from the faucet."

"Not water." E. M. Baxter makes more sense. "Bisnaga juice is a mouth-puckering, mucilaginous, greenish-yellow fluid that would certainly not be chosen for a drink except under the most extreme circumstances."

Most irritable and prickly of Saunder's brood is the cholla. Its limbs, joined like sausages, are covered with spines that glisten in the sun like glass toothpicks. They're savage, these limbs, these baited traps that wait to teach you a lesson you probably have no desire to learn. To brush up against one, ever so lightly, is to disrobe on the spot and get busy with your pliers. Or if you haven't been advised to carry a pair, you remove the limb with your hand. Then you remove it from that hand with the other hand. And so forth, while you slowly fry in the sun.

With theatrical abruptness the weather has changed. The temperature has dropped fifteen degrees, and a breeze has come up behind me, cutting through my ill-chosen hiking shorts. The flowers have pulled their petals into closed packages. The birds have gone quiet and the lizards have abandoned their rocky posts for the day. Miles short of the trail's conclusion on Highway 74, I turn around and cross one arroyo after another, on the run. Another hour of windy walking and I'm back at Hermits Bench, where everything is as it was five hours ago, only a lot less sunny.

With my feet parked in a patio chair, a can of Sprite at my elbow, I doctor my bloody shins and pick cholla spines from my socks. Meanwhile, piles of clouds roll hugely over the mountain, solid towers lit by bolts of lightning. Claps of thunder set off a cannonade of reverberations. And finally, the sky, having withheld its moisture all day, lets loose with fat hesitant splatters, then rain, real rain, heavy, steady rain. Rain sheets off the roof of the patio, throwing the palm trees out of focus. It hurries the most hardy hikers to their cars, their clothes hanging like sodden dishrags. It smells of creosote bushes, slightly medicinal one thinks, clean and strong, fundamentally pleasing.

As the canyon heads toward closing time, the storm rolls off to Arizona. Leaving Millie Fischer to lock up the souvenir hut, I run for the van on the dot of six o'clock. As I regain the smooth pavement, the sky clears, cloud by cloud. I look back and see a rainbow arching bright over the canyon, as Smeaton Chase might have imagined in his highest moments.

FOUR

Reinventing the Village

This December there can be no night-time glory of outdoor Christ-mas trees in the war-darkened land of California. As if in mourn-ing for a once gay and shining night world that has forgotten beauty, thousands of trees that once shamed the splendor of the moon and stars will cast lonely shadows on a dreary, dimmed-out landscape.

—THE DESERT SUN 1942

ESTERDAY'S MAIN STREET is today's Palm Canyon Drive, paved smooth, swept clean, and lined with floodlit palms. From one block to the next, you'll find excellent restaurants with names like Banducci's Bit of Italy, Sorrentino's Seafood, Pepper Thai Cuisine, and Blue Coyote Grill, as well as eating places that are chiefly night clubs, where karaoke singers struggle for an audience in the competition of live bands. There is no shortage here of top-end galleries and souvenir boutiques that do a hectic trade in film, postcards, and "P.S. I Love You" T-shirts. But in all this superfluity, nowhere will you find anything useful—a broom, a bolt of cotton, a sack of beans. All the same, Palm Springs has never given up the habit of thinking of itself as a small, cheery village. Hence the idea behind VillageFest.

Every Thursday night throughout the year, during the

hours from six to ten, barricades block the ordinary bustle of traffic on Palm Canyon Drive. Tonight, with just twenty fleeting days until Christmas, shop windows have sprung to life with displays intended to excite holiday spending. Everything in sight is decked with Christmas regalia, as if to say there's a right way to decorate and this is it. Thousands of fairy lights loop up and down the palm trees. On every lamppost, flags portray traditional holiday scenes. Banners stretched across the street promise the upcoming Parade of Lights and Christmas Craft Show. The result dazzles.

Awnings up, flood lamps switched on, tables wrestled into place, and the twinkling street scene takes on a carnival push and clamor. The various musicians tease us with gusts of tuning up. Half a hundred heavenly aromas compete for our appetites. Already the food stalls are serving, the queues in place and lengthening by the minute.

Any good event makes for a mixed crowd, and so it is here. Jovial pre-Christmas banter fills the cool night air. Greetings take place. Conversations are begun. In the happy hubbub of voices, I hear the fun of foreign tongues: the lilt of French, the whoops from glad groups of Japanese, and half a dozen tongues I can't identify much less understand. I step off the curb and try for a little elbow room. Just glancing around, I see people strolling, shopping, eating, and—a few of them anyway—simply standing still, wondering what to do first. Slowly they detach themselves into portraits: Here's a guy wearing a live boa constrictor looped across his shoulders, like a friend's arm. A freshly peroxided young mom juggles a baby, a cell phone, and a fresh bouquet of flowers. A young couple, dressed in sandals, shorts, and matching T-shirts emblazoned with stylized suns, lick ice cream off each other's cones, as though, this being Palm Springs, it is always summer.

The night has brought out an unusual number of youths, some of whom seem determined to do VillageFest on rollerblades. Youthful skateboarders rocket by, loud and boisterous, their hair dyed acid green, yellow, and pink. The Goth kids fit right in, the whole surly group costumed in black. Their glory lies in body piercing and tattooing; those who display the most are most certain of attention. Even so, they do not draw a second glance from us, the unpunctured and tattoo-free. You can wear anything and do anything in Palm Springs. It's all been seen and done before.

More conspicuous, perhaps, are the police, on bicycles and on horseback. On foot, they make their moves in pairs, giving the impression of friendliness. We are also likely to notice the blue-haired matrons and their matched minidogs, impossibly silky things, groomed to the teeth. "Hi, pooch. Hello, you sweet thing." Far less charming are the rottweilers. "He won't hurt you," one owner tells me, enjoying my anxiety.

Another block and I spot three women in pastel running suits and crisp white perms, grandmothers probably. Moving arm in arm, they form a single unstoppable force that clears a path through the crowd. I stride in their wake, inhaling clouds of competing colognes, a whole back yard of flowers. A gust of fellowship passes between them as slowly they progress, smiling and chatting, through a wonderland of stalls. With sidelong glances at the prices, they finger pottery, wood carvings, and wooden flutes. They dab on samples of hand lotion and offer each other a wrist. They fan hand-painted scarves and reach up the skirts of furry glove-puppets to extract the price tag.

"Oh, isn't this cute" and "Wouldn't that fit right in," they exclaim over this and that.

Up the curb, onto the sidewalk, and abruptly we stop as one grandmother, bending from the waist, begins to read every sidewalk star out loud, as if we are illiterate. "Look, it's Elizabeth Taylor! Look, it's Frank Sinatra!" Well, if Hollywood has it then Palm Springs must have it, or as much of it as we can get. Our Walk of Stars honors people who have contributed in some way to the reputation of Palm Springs, be they pioneer or movie star or just about anybody who wants a star and is willing to plunk down four thousand dollars to get one. The names are as familiar as Marilyn Monroe, Ronald Reagan, Cheeta the Chimp, and as unfamiliar as Chris Alcaide, Pierce Lyden, Betsy Duncan . . . you don't remember Betsy Duncan? If you are looking for the most obscure names in America, look no further than Palm Canyon Drive. "Who's Nellie Coffman?" Before I can properly answer, the grandmothers are borne away by the crowd.

* * *

Mother Coffman, as she was called in deference to her standing in the village, figured largely in the Prickly Pear tapes as the owner of what was once the centerpiece of Main Street. The Desert Inn it was called, and the tourism it offered was personalized and first rate. Its patrons were mostly Easterners, solid, prosperous people who were able to leave their investments and responsibilities for extended periods of time. Upon arriving at the Inn they would rush out of their city clothes and into their blue jeans and Wild West hats. From there the daily routine was all it could be: Mornings on horseback in the canyons, a parade of smiling people with good color in their cheeks, flirting, making friends, doing healthy things in the clean healthy air. Afternoons on the verandah, tipping lazily back on rockers, clicking ice cubes in Nellie Coffman's vehemently nonalcoholic fruit drinks, the air scented with orange blossoms, the music coming softly from a cranked-up Victrola. Then, sometime during the interval between afternoon and evening, newspapers were put down and walking sticks picked up for a stroll into the pink sunset, a miracle that happened every day by the grace of Nellie. And finally, the moment awaited by all arrived: dinner in the DeAnza Room, the tables impeccably set with glistening silver and snowy white linen, the Filipino waiters wafting tantalizing aromas with each pass over the tile floor. The lighting was red candles, the music a string trio. The conversation was cultured, the drinking discreet. Dress was formal and in good taste; Nellie saw to that! Tacked up in each guest room were euphemistic notices announcing that ladies expecting to use the dining room must dress with no more than the "prescribed number of lumbar vertebrae" exposed.

Nellie Coffman was the soul of goodness, according to nearly all the stories I have read. Even in that age when charitable work was expected of influential women, she was remarkable for her efforts on behalf of the village poor. She was the Welfare Society, in person, the Public School System, in person. She was a "one-woman city council," who held the reins of the village in a tight grip, a "self-appointed chamber of commerce," who almost single-handedly put Palm Springs on the map. The only way to have stopped growth was to do away with Mother Coffman.

In the fall of 1909, forty-two-year-old Nellie arrived at Seven Palms with the elder of her two sons and her husband

Dr. Coffman (he would be her husband for only five more years, even though divorce was a monstrous thing in those days). All the money they had scraped together didn't amount to much, but back then, as one of Nellie's biographers is at pains to point out, you could have bought ten square miles, including the village itself, for fifty thousand dollars. Agua Caliente it was called. You could count the white residents on your fingers, with a digit to spare.

Coming from Indiana by way of Texas and Colorado, in large part aboard a covered wagon, Nellie eyed the infant village as if she meant to eat it. With $2,000 down, a $2,500 mortgage, and a 90-day grocery credit, she opened her boarding house cum sanitarium. It was a small spread at first, *nestled*, as they say, in the lee of the San Jacintos, infinitely snug and wholesome. Up to twelve guests were quartered in homey canvas cottages and aired on porches salvaged out of what had been an old hay barn in a former life. Pitched beneath pleasant, familiar trees, each cottage had an oil heater, a kerosene lamp, a wash basin, a slop jar, and a little pig-iron bedstead heated with hot bricks whenever there was a hint of cold in the air. White pickets fenced a farmyard of chickens, one milk cow, and one pampered bull that had come into Nellie's possession on the installment plan.

Mother Coffman was a humdinger of a cook, that's what everyone said. Her philosophy was "The way to every man's heart is through his stomach," and the philosophy was there in her lamb chops, creamed potatoes, smoking-hot soda biscuits, and rich country gravy. It was there in her manzanita berry jam and the cool sweet butter she churned herself, giving the porch a pleasant touch of domesticity. Indeed, pictures show a dumpling of a woman with rosy, rice-powdered cheeks plumped on her own good cooking. Dressed in a fresh apron and a serviceable sunbonnet, sturdy shoes under sturdier ankles, she looks like the essence of good-hearted womanhood. Except that behind those gold-rimmed specs were eyes that could find their target at a hundred yards.

Hotelier "Auntie" Pearl McManus was another tough-minded mover and shaker, likewise up to her neck in local issues. As such, she often strayed into the line of fire of Nellie's long-range eyes. Theirs was a private feud that displayed itself in public as "frigid politeness."

After laboring through Nellie's biography, I quickly tired of Pearl's "generous nature," her ability to speak "firmly and with finality to tycoons, promoters, and lawmakers." *Auntie* didn't fit her at all. She was not a lovable little old lady. She was a woman of "strong opinion," a "true sophisticate" with an old-money equestrienne look and a fondness for pink stucco. Because it was hard to stay awake, much less take responsible notes, I focused my attention on the photographs. Here was little Pearlie and her burro . . . Miss Pearl, under a load of chestnut hair, at the Marlborough School for young ladies in Los Angeles . . . Mrs. Pearl McManus in a big rodeo hat, her hair, now taken in another direction, cropped short like a man's . . . Auntie Pearl sitting easily in the saddle on a tall, lively horse. We see her face weathered by the sun, her eyes narrowed with what might be construed as scorn. Her lips are pressed together in a tight, unyielding seal, the eyes joined with the lips in a look of authority that seems to deny she had ever been young. We have Pearl on the terrace of her pink mansion, her face creased with one of her migraines, as if the photographer had called her forth from her sick bed so he might record the scene.

A young woman when Palm Springs was young, Pearl focused all her ambition on real estate. She collected acres like stamps, until she became the largest single landowner in the village. The daughter of early developer John Guthrie McCallum, Pearl became a developer in her own right, selling off McCallum's original holdings piece by piece (in her last days, by village standards, she was worth a bundle). "Even now, on occasion," she said in an interview several years before her death,

> I can mount my horse, ride to some promontory and look far out over the desert, sometimes in the daytime, and sometimes at night when your houselights twinkle with the stars, and even though you have true titles and deeds to your home, your lands, and your ranches, so long as I am here on the desert, in my fancy, in my love, and in my friendship, every palm, every house, every tumbleweed, every grain of sand and branch of mesquite is my own, all my own.

It comes as no surprise that the Mmes. Coffman and McManus tended to put an intellectual and social distance between each other. After all, the well-established Desert Inn with its clientele of long standing was but a stone's throw from Pearl's new three-storied Oasis Hotel. Built by Lloyd Wright, son of Frank Lloyd, the Oasis sported a rooftop terrace, the near-mandatory bell tower, a swimming pool, and an emerald lawn "whereon a brazier holds a cheerful bonfire and a spirit of substantial comfort pervades." Food was served as a sort of diversion in a ninety-foot-long dining room built around two cottonwood trees, their trunks providing a unique centerpiece, their branches a romantic spread of leaves. As Nellie must have noted with dismay, Pearl's Oasis lorded it over the Inn, made it look frumpy.

When in good form, which was often, Nellie Coffman could not be outclassed. As the size and status of her clientele grew, so grew the Desert Inn. She put her whole weight behind it, and the weight of her two grown sons, bringing all thirty-five acres up to snuff in Mission Revival loveliness, with red-tiled roofs, hand-hewn beams, granite fireplaces, potted palms, and hand-crafted wicker furniture. Entrance was now gained through an imposing iron gate, putting the old white pickets to shame. The canvas cottages came down and a cluster of new rooms, suites, and apartments rose in their place. A deep, palatial porch was added, and here Heifetz performed his magic when he was in town (if you were a guest and you had talent, you were obliged to entertain well into the late hours, Nellie saw to *that*). Tennis courts were added, and an Olympic-size swimming pool where frolicking nymphs put aside their late Victorian taboos and wore bathing suits that set tongues wagging, sometimes in admiration, sometimes in scorn.

It's easy to imagine Mother Coffman bustling around her spanking-new kitchen, making a production out of dinner preparation, a little ceremony of stirring, sniffing, tasting. In her new dining salon, glowing in harmonies of polished wood, there she was smothering you in hospitality, hovering over your table, pointing out on the menu items Chef Woon did especially well. Out of the kitchen came the fresh lobster cocktail and fruit supreme. Out came the southern chicken okra, the mountain brook trout, the grilled spring lamb chops, the braised suckling pig, the baked calf sweetbreads dressed with appropriate sauces . . . and goodness knows what else.

When at last faces were lifted from the dinner plates, out came the finger bowls and desserts of boundless joy and form.

The gardens of the Desert Inn, tricked into riotous bloom, rambled agreeably through what had become a veritable village within the village, with its own private school, brokerage office, coffee shop, and art gallery. A barber shop, perfumed with pomade and shampoo, stood under Nellie's same hospitable roof, along with a dormitory for the Inn's employees, all of them enormously eager to please. There were public spaces reserved at the Inn for civic meetings and ordinary socializing—Nellie Coffman, the charitable agent of events. Why go out for anything? Should you need medical attention, room 326 was the office of Dr. Henry S. Reid. Should an invitation to a charity ball come winging your way, the Inn was there to dress your hair in the latest fashion—a bouffant, perhaps, or a mass of sausage curls. At the mention of gowns, you would be shown layers of satin and lace, a gold lamé evening bag, a rope of pearls, a hat—just a little something in velvet, with a bit of trim: grosgrain, feathers, a single rose.

All social activity was now "under the guidance of a capable director"—the ad-writers were quick to catch up with Nellie's new way of doing things. As were a dazzling succession of guests that included Eddie Cantor, Dolores Del Rio, Charlie Chaplin, Rudolph Valentino, Jack Benny, William S. Hart, Gilbert Roland, cartoonist Jimmy Swinnerton, a dimpled moppet named Shirley Temple, W. K. Kellogg of the toasted corn flake factory, King Gillette of the American Safety Razor Company ("no stropping, no honing, just lather and shave"), and A. P. Giannini, founder of Bank of America. Nellie, you see, was particularly careful about allowing in no person whose character had not undergone a thorough investigation.

So there it was, the Desert Inn, so dear to every village heart. Except that it proved no more durable than Nellie herself. In 1967, ten years after her death, it was bulldozed into oblivion and hauled ignobly to the Coachella Valley landfill, signaling the end of a grand era. And then a further insult: The bareness of the site inspired developers to assemble something really ugly—a multilayered parking structure, a multistoried hotel, and a shopping mall designed without regard for nostalgia. The mall was never a commercial success, did not draw the expected throngs; hence it is waiting to be demolished (as I write) and rebuilt to a different pattern.

The same blind indifference to village heritage ended elegant dining at the Oasis. But miraculously, the hotel lobby, suites, and bell tower have survived, although waiting their turn for restoration or destruction. The workmanship is still obvious—the hotel's fine design and elegant construction. The decrepitude is almost grand—the peeling turquoise trim, the gently decaying pink stucco. The hotel's basic fabric retains a prosperous look, as if the arrival of the next train will restore it to glory.

* * *

Eight o'clock, and above the VillageFest scene, the Oasis bell tower gongs the Westminster chime, stroke of hour, and "Silent Night" (actually, it's a recorded arrangement, the volume turned way up). At street level, amplifying systems are working with a vengeance, way beyond the limits of city code: country western and Dixieland in one ear, rock 'n roll and rhythm 'n blues in the other. Frankly, this falls short of musical bliss, but it isn't Venice Beach either, where any joker can set up a microphone. You can't sing at VillageFest if you can't sing. You have to audition. You have to be talented. Ron O'Riley furnishes a fair example as he works his way through the entire repertoire of Roy Orbison. Drop a dollar in the guitar case before you leave. That kind of applause has real meaning.

The next block brings Fabiano. Punching the play button for his background music, he heaves himself into song; suddenly the Caribbean isn't so far away. Next comes energetic Rudy, the Harvard Street Singer who breaths fresh life and volume into it all. If there are any false notes, most of Palm Springs will know.

A crowd forms a semicircle three deep around Rocco, a grandfatherly gentleman whose slapstick humor runs to false eyebrows and a Jimmy Durante nose. Rocco's frantic, he's passionate, God knows he's loud enough. He plays the harmonica, the kazoo, the banjo, the washboard, and the cymbals, in no particular order—you can't believe it's just one man. The zinger in his act is a wind-up monkey on drums. The monkey is every bit as amusing as Rocco and makes just as much money.

Clearly the food stalls know what they are doing; an inexhaustible flow of money pours into their tills. Everything a hungry visitor could want is taken into account by somebody. Mentally, I consume a meatball sandwich, a slice of pizza, a beef kabob enlivened by a secret sauce that remains a secret despite my efforts. That keeps me going until I reach the stall with the blue awning and checkered tablecloth. Minutes later a chicken pita bulges from my fingers, the sour cream dressing spilling down my chin and shirtfront ("top secret" was the reply when I asked what else went into the dressing). Next I attack a little see-through-thin crepe, a bit of heaven with strawberries and whipped cream. On and on I go, making up for lost meals. Any minute now the belt will run out of holes.

Up ahead lies the farmer's market, an ambling passage in which half an hour might pass in the purchase of a few melons. Behind tables heaped with the triumphs of Southern California agriculture, farmers straight from the fields await your order. They offer noble ears of corn, tall stalks of Brussels sprouts, strawberries in astonishing sizes, and luscious clusters of grapes ripened to rubies. Unlike me, a few fussy customers are not content merely to look before buying. They must find the most tender, the juiciest, the best. They sniff the tomatoes and squeeze the avocados. They poke suspiciously at a cluster of mushrooms that look highly poisonous, not at all like the civilized mushrooms sold in stores. Someone takes a kiwi from the wrong place in a stacked pyramid, and kiwis in twos and threes tumble to the ground.

Having stowed in my rucksack far more than I had intended to purchase, I set off for Starbucks, ostensibly to relax over a cup of coffee, but really to escape from VillageFest, the riot of sound, the tumble of tempting food. I pay the bill, locate a vacant table among the dozens arranged on the sidewalk, and in a momentary island of quiet, bend to the vapor of my espresso. Pushing aside my cup, I settle down to my notebook, the lines smeared with chocolate, glistening with grease, and sticky with honey from the evening's research. I thought this would be a good place to collect my thoughts, but it's no good at all. The animated conversation from a table of four captures my attention. The middle-aged couple, having just done a week in Los Angeles, are talking in tandem about muggings and murders, a seamless dialogue which neither requires nor allows any contribution from the listeners. "One night we were leaving our hotel and . . ." That kind of story. And to keep the ball rolling, this kind of sequel: "You think that's bad? Then we were driving through Westwood when . . ." They shake their heads and add another tale of distress.

Conversations come and go among other tables around me. The topics touch the usual bases: a great meal had somewhere, how bad the food was somewhere else, the great weather here, how bad the weather is somewhere else. Apparently, people are being frozen to death in New York, blown off their feet in Chicago, and drowned in West Palm Beach. If I were seeking a vacation spot, I'd definitely pick Palm Springs.

* * *

During the era of Mother Coffman and Auntie Pearl, Palm Springs, like most tourist towns, had its landmark, its Eiffel Tower, where the tourist could say, when he reached it, "Now I'm *really* here." Such a place was the hot mineral spring, the *springs* of Palm Springs. Here, a block east of Starbucks, the *palms* of Palm Springs rose above a pool of water that surfaced at 110 degrees from a deep aquifer on the Palm Canyon Fault (the fault is dormant, no longer the scene of appreciable activity—for now). Owned historically and currently by the Agua Caliente Band of Cahuilla Indians—the hot water Indians—the spring was considered magical, curative, worthy of the tourist buck. And indeed the tourists came, along with the villagers without bathtubs in their homes, intent only on getting clean. There they all were to be seen, Mother Coffman among them, a dowdy come-as-you-are party in bathrobes and bedroom slippers.

Smeaton Chase took the waters and found the experience delightful, the weird sensation produced by the gulpings and gur-glings of the spring [and the] added excitement of guess-ing whether the rickety little hut would fall to pieces while you were taking your bath or would spare you and collapse over the next comer.

The spring itself was a pit of clean white sand (or a primor-dial soup of mud, depending on your source) encircled by a rough platform with two "friendly timbers" across the open-ing that you used to lower yourself into the water. Whether there was a bottom to this spring, somewhere deep down its spooky depths, was anybody's guess. The notion had teased the villagers into dropping a plumb line, but at six hundred feet the weight continued to dangle uselessly in the abyss. Drop your watch, they warned, and it falls clear to China.

Chase again:

You may bask in the clear water on the surface of the pool, or, if you want all the fun you can get for your money, you may lower yourself into the very mouth of the spring where the mixture comes gurgling up. This will yield you (especially at night and by candle-light) a novel and somewhat shuddery experience . . . As you sink, the sand gulps and gurgles about you with strange, uncanny noises, and you probably hold on rather nerv-ously to your friendly timbers. But you soon find that there is no need for alarm, for the good, reliable principle of specific gravities checks your descent before you sink to the armpits; and there you are, snug enough, hanging like a small cork in the neck of the big bottle . . . As the sand quakes and shudders around you, you no doubt wonder just what is going on down below, and would like to know how far down "below" extends.

Picture Chase emerging from the spring, his poisons per-spired away, his body so warm and relaxed he can barely stand. He returns the key to Madam B., "who spares a moment from the eternal basket to remark, with a fat laugh, 'You likeum bath, all right.'" (With all respect to Chase, I wonder why it is that early writers tended to represent Indians as monosyllabic blockheads.)

Although this ancient spring still exists, still bubbles up mineral-rich from the ancient fissure, in order to ensure a continuous supply regardless of use, the water is now stored in two monstrous underground tanks from which it is distributed via miles of pipe to thirty-five sunken tubs. As you would ex-pect, Chase's rickety hut has given way to massive concrete beams and an embellishment of terrazzo tile. In its present in-carnation, the Spa offers its moneyed guests a series of New Age frills. A nude sunbath on the rooftop gymnasium is well worth having and goes well with a hot plunge in the whirlpool. I also recommend a private massage and cooldown. The eucalyptus fumes will clear the cobwebs from your head.

Adjoining the Spa, and totally at odds with its opulence, is a white circus tent that holds a maze of slot machines. There's an almost deliberate impermanence to the tent, as if it could be disassembled with a moment's warning and spirited away into the desert. The interior is poorly lit, claustrophobic, and gloomy. I imagine a grease fire erupting in the kitchen and having to claw my way out through aisles of slack-jawed in-somniacs perched on stools, trying out their systems. To lure these people in off the street, the tribe has circumvented the city's ordinance and erected a big sign that flashes a mess of scarlet neon messages: Jackpots Daily . . . Cowboy BBQ . . . Breakfast for a Buck. I, for one, would not be sad to see the sign, the tent, the whole shebang fold up and the land turned into a dog park or a community vegetable garden. Never happen of course.

* * *

Roughly eight blocks west of the Spa, and a world away, lies a small cemetery where the old families have tucked away several generations of loved ones. You would surely miss the place if you didn't come with a purpose. Nothing announces what goes on here, except a low wall built of irregular stones that is perhaps the oldest artifact around. If only you could make the notion of peace into a tangible object, it would look like this place. The morbidity of death simply evaporates in the sunny atmosphere. Yet hardly anyone comes.

Some of the graves bear ornate gravestones, with perhaps a picture, a poignant bit of Bible verse, a potful of flowers that will never die. Others bear simple, polished plaques, recessed below the sod to make mowing easier. And a few bear plain old rocks inscribed with nothing but the bare facts: Stewart 1909. Mexican Woman. Our Beloved Mysterious Hermit. Unknown—this last grave being that of an indigent corpse, unloved and alone. I imagine that even in life some of the villagers were referred to not by name but by the role they played—the Mayor, the Town Drunk, the Village Idiot.

So many of the village dead were buried thousands of miles from where they were born. Here lies Cornelia White, born in New York and buried beside her sister Florilla White. Here lies J. Smeaton Chase, born in England and buried beside his wife,

Isabel, the third White sister. Here lies Welwood Murray, born in Scotland and buried beside his ample wife, Elizabeth Erskine Murray, who died knowing what hard frontiers do to women and what women then do to the men who keep them there. Here lies Otto Adler, born in the Netherlands and buried beside his wife, Louisa, who, according to her epitaph, "died of grief caused by a neighbor."

The Adlers were the Red Front Hotel, the Red Front Grocery, and the *Red Front Store News*, where ads shared column space with a smattering of personals:

Figs are being shipped out by wagon loads to the Los Angeles market.

Sorry to hear Mr. Bisbee lost one of his valuable mules this week just as he began shipping grapes and needed him. Inconsistency your name is mule.

Red Front Hotel: Open Every Day. Screen Tent Rooms 50c. Open Air Dining Room. Meals at all Hours. Chicken Dinner 50c.

Am thankful I'm not a girl. Am thankful we licked the Indians. Am thankful we have a Red Front Store where we can buy fire works, soda water, ice cream, and candy—amen

Here lies Harry Mutascio, born in Italy and buried beside his wife, Josephine. A Prickly Pear interviewer went after their son Nick for the story:

In those days the church would let you have land if you promised a son to the church. Dad did not want to become a priest, so . . . he just gathered up what little money he could and came to America.

As simple as that. But the statement conjures up other images: a frightening transatlantic ordeal, the enormous mass of New York suddenly on top of you, the smudge of factory smokestacks, the tenement blocks with no space to breathe, the sidewalks swarming with struggling immigrants not long removed from Ellis Island. Was there really a place in that city for Harry Mutascio?

Anyone who thinks of California as a land of fresh starts and new beginnings might think of Harry and his new wife and their memories of living in the Bronx, the grim images they took with them to Palm Springs. Although living expenses in 1922 are absurd to the point of incredibility when place beside the figures of today, upon arriving in the village, Harry's first thought was of employment. Unfortunately, he was limited in the work he could do, partly because he was unskilled and partly because he barely knew the English language. On the other hand, he was strong and could hold up his end of any odd job. Seven Palms was as good a place as any for that kind of work. So in season he met the trains and distributed the arrivals among the hotels—along with whatever they had brought with them, their children and grandchildren, their nurses, nannies, and maids, their bulging bags, hat boxes, vanity cases, and steamer trunks separated from the heap: "Those two, and that one, and the big one over there. And there should be one more." In the off-season, to keep his growing family fed, he spent long hours of sweat in Auntie Pearl's citrus grove, Harry in his undershirt, plucking the weeds it then became his job to haul away. It was Indian work at Indian pay, and it was ten cents an hour less than Mexican pay. Harry had not packed up and come west to work for these wages. How much he was giving up in dignity and freedom when other people controlled his labor. Harry believed in himself, and in his special version of the American dream. The good old U.S. of A., land of opportunity. In such a country, a man could find real work, be his own boss. He could open, say, a cafe smack in the middle of the village. He, Harry Mutascio, the new Harry Mutascio, could profit from America's new eagerness for Italian cooking.

Summer might not be the best time to build a cafe in the desert. Even under the best conditions, masonry work is tedious, as anyone who has ever laid bricks can testify. In order to save money, Harry went a step further and made his own bricks, incorporating into the cement quantities of his dripping sweat. Bred to a temperate, maritime climate, Harry didn't know that hot could be so hot as he clambered up and down the ladder, carrying bricks and mortar to his brother-in-law on the wall. I never knew Harry in person, of course, but in my former life, during the foundation stage of our Idaho cabin-building, I assisted my husband's masonry efforts. The job was every bit as tedious and boring as you might expect. Like Harry, I was never a builder to begin with, and I got steadily less ambitious as the project wore on. Then one day in November, when I was pretty much reduced to standing around shivering, the falling snow freezing in my hair, I abandoned Stew and went indoors, to his great relief I'm sure. And I am just as sure that there came a day in August, about midway along Harry's sizable project, when he could be overheard muttering to himself in various and rough Italian phrasings, but basically, "Why in God's name bricks? How did I get myself into this?"

When all was said and done, Harry's Palm Springs Cafe was not so much a place as *the* place of village life. It was the sweet pungency of tomato sauce bubbling with oregano. It was the tinkle and chink of glass and plate. It was the clicking of billiard balls and the chilling hum of the air conditioner, a metal monster that Harry had fabricated with coils salvaged from a walk-in freezer. The a/c operated with freezing competence until someone opened the door and the hot air bellowed in, wiping out all the work it had done for the past hour.

Harry treated his customers as if they had not so much entered a business as strayed into his home, which in fact they had, the building having quarried its way into living quarters in back. You couldn't separate the business from the family. Harry's wife, Josephine, with heavy dark hair and lips used to giving orders, controlled the till as she controlled the squad of juvenile assistants she kept on the move, filling salt shakers, emptying ashtrays, waiting tables, bussing dishes, washing pots and pans.

> People liked my father and mother, you know. They knew that they were hard working people and they served good food. My father would get up at five in the morning and work all day 'till twelve, one o'clock that night and was back up again at five. There was no such thing as a vacation. There were no days off. We had it twenty-four hours a day, seven days a week.

Harry was making it in the good old American way, attaining a success unimaginable in his old, forsaken life in Italy. The lunch counter with its dozen or so swivel chairs evolved into a real restaurant, and he opened a hotel, which he also built. The eager young immigrant who had been Mutascio the hired hand evolved into the comfortable leading citizen of Mutascio the businessman.

* * *

Harry's story is a classic Palm Springs biography, as Palm Springs in Harry's time was a classic model of front-porch America, a community where distances were measured in blocks not miles, and latchstrings, not locks, held the doors closed, as if there were not a crook in the world. Marriages stayed together, mortgages were paid, and cases of gout were cured. Milk came warm and unpasteurized from the Jerseys corralled in village yards. Vegetables and fruits came fresh, in their various seasons, from old Pop Gunn's peddler wagon. Eggs came fresh, or reasonably fresh, from a family whose chickens laid more than the family could eat.

Social life revolved around benefits, every fund producing its own community dance, chuck wagon dinner, and moon-light ride led by a cowboy skilled in singing. There were rodeos, and for weeks the barber shop did no business while the men let their whiskers grow. There was a proper little downtown, but it was so small you could see the whole length as you approached. Walk fifteen minutes and you came to wide-open desert.

Old Main Street was wonderfully devoid of glamour. It could easily be caught napping on a Sunday afternoon, the yellow dogs, at least five or six of the pack, sprawled in the middle of things, chewing their fleas; the tousled chickens scratching out a living in the dust, chasing grasshoppers back into the fields; the horses pawing the dirt, their day devoted to switching flies; the burros nodding in the shade, occasionally letting loose a volley of hysterical shrieks. Accounts testify to a good many animals on the loose, neighing and braying, lowing and bleating, and ever alert for gates left ajar. The horses and burros could be easily caught if anyone cared to catch them, but the mules hadn't been ridden for years. "There is some instinct in these brutes," Smeaton Chase tells us, "that guides them unerringly for miles on any errand of depredation, yet drives them away from where their presence is desired."

Even more troublesome were the rawboned cattle, of no singular breed, that wandered freely up and down Main, sometimes back and forth if, in their bovine stupidity, they couldn't make up their mind where to go. The damage they did, mainly at night and usually in haphazard bunches, was far more infuriating than the damage wild things did, as well as more extensive. Wild things generally have a right to do what they do, even as you have a right to stop them. But the Indians owned these errant cows, and they were obliged to control them now that the land was becoming thickly settled by whites. The Indians felt otherwise. Fences were expensive and they saw no need for them—even as their cattle were kicking over garbage cans, raising hell with the patio furniture, and wreaking major havoc in the hard-worked gardens. All of which created an uproar of shouting and shooting appropriate to those days in a frontier community. I don't suppose that anyone could say for certain whether those slabs of juice-oozing steaks that turned up barbecued and delicious at those chuck wagon dinners were or were not from tribal cows, but all was fair in this.

Old Main Street had no sidewalks, and street lighting was left "in the hands of mother nature." Other amenities were so few they, too, are best described in the negative. There was no street maintenance beyond a one-man service run by Henry P. Lotz, whose fixed assets amounted to a broom, a shovel, and a much battered sedan with big garbage cans wired to the front and back bumpers. There was no waste disposal beyond Caesar Spalleti, an Italian immigrant who drove his truck around to everyone's driveway, then hung out at the post office and handed out his bills. Some of the old people who lived on the outskirts of town simply heaved off their tin cans, sprung mattresses, and dead dogs on a stretch of desert not far away, but not on their own place either. There the stuff would stack up for weeks and months and years, rusting and rotting among the creosote bushes and No Dumping signs, a paradise for rats and flies. Then when land grew scarce and it mattered more, a county ordinance came out saying that you could be fined, even jailed, for "the placing, dumping, depositing, or throwing of rubbish, bottles, tin cans, wire, automobile parts, bodies of old wagons or buggies, or other vehicles in whole or in part, citrus fruit, deciduous fruit, vegetables, junk, etc., etc., etc." Even if you were an old person.

Although fires were common enough, the young village had no fire department, or rather, nothing you could properly call a fire department. When funding comes from benefit dances, you can't expect much beyond the basics: a handful of volunteers called fire laddies, a two wheeled affair called a chemical cart (it looked like a civil war cannon painted red), and an agreement between neighbors to couple their garden hoses. Here's how it worked: A telephone had been installed outside the Desert Inn Garage, and a horn on a nearby pole. Whoever heard the phone ring would answer it, then reach over and pull the rope that blew the horn that told the laddies where to go. One blast meant the north end of town. Two blasts meant the south. Three blasts (downtown) and all the dogs joined in, the terrible, contagious howling spreading from dog to dog in rising octaves that came so close on the heels of the horn they were like an extension of it. All this alarming commotion caused the laddies to grab their helmets and hatchets and rush from their homes and offices like stirred-up ants out of a nest. Meanwhile all the village looked on, counting the blasts—one, two, three. Fire Chief Bill Leonesio remembers, although not fondly: "We had no masks, no oxygen tanks, we just did it the hard way . . . went in there and took as much as you could, came out and the next man would take as much as he could."

At some point in its evolution, it became the fire department's duty to announce twelve noon with a long blast of the horn. This is how Village Time worked: The laddie on duty would call the telephone company for the correct time. Then he would synchronize the station clock in preparation for the noon blast. The trouble was that sometimes the blast would be five, ten, even fifteen minutes late; a volunteer was as subject to forgetfulness as the next person. But eventually the laddie would pull the rope that blew the horn that announced the noon, and everyone within earshot would stop and reset his watch to the correct time. The telephone company, located next door to the fire department, would also hear the horn and, you guessed it, reset their clock.

The young village had no banks; thus banking was conducted in Riverside, half a day's drive away. The village had no courts or juries, nor any need for them. There was no crime, and so no police force beyond one old unarmed deputy named Dodds, who inspired fear in no one. Every Wednesday

Dodds would wander down from Banning to share a few beers curbside with the village loafers. If anybody had a community grievance, he'd go talk to Dodds. Strictly private squabbles were settled privately.

To be accurate, I should say there was no *serious* crime. There were the vagrants, of course, indigent strangers who strayed over from the subculture of hoboes camped between journeys at Seven Palms. That they stole underwear off clotheslines was a common complaint. Beyond that they raided chicken coops for the mulligan they cooked over campfires and washed down with cheap red wine. You knew who they were by their sour smell, and by their skin, darker even than their dirty clothes. Just as you knew how fast the railroad bulls would grab them, run them a safe distance out of town, and give them the freedom of the West.

City planning was as distinctly Wild West as law enforcement; that is, there was no city planning. There were no planning boards or zoning ordinances to annoy the villagers. There were no rules, like houses go here, shops over there, offices here, restaurants there; you could put a grocery store in a residential neighborhood where it was most needed and within easy walking distance. It was Dodge City, complete with hitching posts, false-fronted hotels (like those made famous by western movies), and a few low adobes that had no claim to fashion.

Adobe was as good as anything you could get from a sawmill. But you had to get the mix right. Too much clay and the bricks would crack; too little clay and the bricks would crumble. Even when everything went right, it was a killing labor, as witnessed by Marshall McKinney. With the critical eye of a fourteen-year-old, he watched his father help prepare the adobe for Dr. Kocher's pharmacy, the Mortar and Pestle.

First, Dad plowed the red clay, or scratched it. It was too hard to plow. Then he ran water over it to soften it. They wet it and scratched it again and again until it could be plowed. Then they made it into a big mud puddle and scattered a lot of straw on it. Then they plowed it, and walked in it with the horses until it was well mixed, and just the right muddiness. Then they shoveled the clay-straw mud into 12x18x4 inch forms and left them to dry. In three or four days the clay had dried and shrunk enough for the forms to be lifted off and refilled. It took only another week or so in the dry desert air [until] they were solid enough to be tipped up on edge for complete and faster drying. In a month or so, they were quite dry and ready to be built into walls.

In the front part of his pharmacy, Dr. John Jacob Kocher performed his mysteries, grinding bunches of dried this and dried that into potions that tasted impressively bad. For every little ailment, he had a powder, he had a pill, a cream, a paste, a plaster—none of which can hardly have done more than psychological good. The idea was to make you feel that attention was being paid, something was being done. But basically, disease was an inescapable fact of life that had to be endured.

In the back part of his pharmacy, Dr. Kocher brought people into the world, ushered them out, and did all kinds of things to them in between. It was commonly said that if the patient lived, the doctor had saved him; if the patient died, the doctor had been called too late. And what about his losses, there being no mortician in the village to rely on for disposal, if that peculiar situation can be so described? Well, when Grandfather passed away (typically from TB), you began the arrangements by sending a telegram to the cabinet-maker Mr. Wiefels in Banning. Then you wrapped Grandfather in a blanket and sent him off to the Seven Palms station. There he was met by Mr. Wiefels, put into a coffin, and taken by train to Banning, where his waxen features would be decently composed. Then the coffin, and whatever it now contained, was sent back to Seven Palms. From there it was delivered to a rectangular hole pickaxed through the rocky earth of the little graveyard, the One Mule Stage serving as hearse. When the church bell tolled, all work in the village stopped. There was no question that Grandfather had belonged to a caring community.

Dr. Kocher's pharmacy shared the leafy shade of Main Street with Bunkers Garage, a big functional building with a dirt floor, a pit for easy access to undercarriages, and a glass-headed gasoline pump where you could "fill her up" and get directions at the same time. At this point, the Prickly Pear pioneers always introduce Zaddie Bunker, a woman who had Woman's Lib a good many years before it went public. By all accounts, Zaddie would have been a remarkable woman in any era. Improbably dressed in bib-top overalls, from whose greasy recesses she was at any moment likely to produce a wrench, she took automobiles apart and put them together again, for which she has earned my gushing admiration.

With only four automobiles in the village, Zaddie's rate of a dollar an hour didn't hold body and soul together for long. But with Zaddie anything was possible. Notably, and controversially, she became the first woman in California to earn a chauffeur's license, after which she made it her business to haul anything and everything that would fit into her big seven-passenger Benham: passengers, baggage, and mailbags to and from the Seven Palms station, ice from Banning to the Desert Inn, gasoline from Bunkers Garage to the tiny airstrip brushed out of the sand. Flying field it was called, one office, one hanger, a few little prop planes.

Over the years, without doing much about it, Zaddie had dreamed of flying. Finding a pilot willing to teach her was itself an event. Zaddie was a little rattle-headed, they claimed. And she was a woman, an *old* woman. As for discouraging Zaddie, being old and female never did. Her determination to fly was nothing if not serious, and in San Bernardino she finally received her flight instructions and, undoubtedly, the respect she so richly deserved. Three years later, at age sixty, she earned her private pilot's license, and her multi-engine license three years after that. For the rest of her vigorous elder years, she flew a succession of brave little planes, the words Zaddie's Rocking Chair painted on the fuselage, giving her a boost.

Giving in to old age never crossed Zaddie's mind. "Zaddie Sets Off on World Flight" cried the press. "Flying Great-Grandmother Wins Cross-Country Air Race." At seventy-three, when she might have taken to her slippers and easy chair, she astounded reporters again by passing the rigorous Air Force physical for jet pilots. "I came from a family of long-lived Missouri farmers," she explained. "I have never had any minor bad habits. I never wanted to drink anything with liquor in it and I never smoked cigarettes." Then came her greatest moment of fame: Zaddie, now an honorary colonel in the Air Force, sitting at the controls of an F-100 Super-sabre jet, zooming to more than eight hundred miles an hour. "It was the greatest ride I ever had in my life. Except for the needles jumping, I didn't realize anything had happened." Again she galvanized the press: "Supersonic Zaddie Breaks the Sound Barrier."

Even in her ageless eighties, Zaddie couldn't be stopped. Further to bemuse the young pilots of the village, she applied for duty on the Apollo flight to the moon. "Colonel 'Shorty' Powers gave me forty-five minutes in that space capsule simulator," she reported. But, alas, no moon shot for Zaddie. "I know I could have done it, I could have done it," she said. And not one person doubted that she could. In 1969 she died much respected.

* * *

Full membership in Zaddie's young village meant membership in the Saint Florian Church, a chaste white clapboard with a bell that rang a pleasant Sunday peacefulness over Main Street. For any stray visitor who might be persuaded to stop over for the night, there were the usual mom-and-pop hotels plus a few motor courts that every villager had an opinion about, a point of view that sooner or later included the adjective *ugly*. For visitors and villagers alike, there were nine riding stables, some of which had been started with mavericks whisked away from the Indian herds. There were also a few tennis courts, squeezed between the graveyard and the mountains, and half a golf course, absurdly wet and green. (Dr. Kocher's orders included walking in short stretches amid quantities of fresh air. Given that everyone was almost frenziedly active outdoors anyway, his orders seem superfluous.)

Above all, when you think of Main Street in Zaddie's time, no two words are as suggestive as Lykkens Store, an institution so vanished today it might have belonged to the Stone Age.

Here Carl Lykken, lately from Los Angeles and Mexico, combined the forces of a general store, a Western Union office, and a post office, where mail from every stratum of society was sorted by name (envelopes were addressed simply *Village*, without street numbers, because there weren't any). Lykkens was a gathering place where you could walk in at almost any hour and encounter old friends, and when they asked about your health they actually waited for your answer, as if you had just had a leg taken off. If you were a kid running an errand for your mom, you might get to visiting with half a dozen friends running errands for their moms. You'd look at the dollar bill clutched in your hand and forget what you had come for.

Lykkens Store boasted the first sidewalk in town. By sidewalk, I mean a small section of sidewalk, with a roof to shade the window displays and the small knot of loafers who hung around on the off chance something might happen. Lykkens had the first telephone in town, a clunky wooden wall instrument with a crank, a ringing gismo, and a battery that had the potential to dry up, overflow, or explode. When the rotary dial came into being in 1921, with a wheel and ten finger holes, a number in each hole, the telephone company had to spend eight paragraphs in the new village directory explaining how the thing worked, and four more paragraphs explaining the use and abuse of the shared telephone line. Suddenly, from the privacy of your home, you could nose in on other homes and thereby attain a furtive insight into lives at once more mysterious and more humdrum than your own.

What that left of the telephone directory was one page of four-digit numbers, in which Beatrice Horst listed her residence as "bet Park and Spring on Tahquitz" and Miss T. C.

Chariteir, Masseuse advertised herself as being available on the "cor Lemon and Main." In those dear days before the voice of Visa and Sears spoiled the dinner hour, the ringing of the telephone was musical prelude to a happy invitation that would enliven your weekend.

Most of all, Lykkens was a supply depot for the necessities and little luxuries of civilized life. The food processing giants provided Carl with a cornucopia of products. Armour and Swift dominated the shelves of canned meats, Heinz and Campbell the canned fruits and vegetables, Post and Kellogg the cereals, Kraft and Borden the dairy. You could find just about everything in Lykkens: coffee and crackers in barrels and bins; cornmeal, flour, and dried beans in large sacks; lemon snaps, Tootsie Rolls, and Campfire marshmallows in tins big enough to give the whole village a roast. As it turned out, the lard pails meant all too much to the Indians, as did the bottles of vanilla extract, one of which contained almost as much alcohol as a Manhattan cocktail.

You could go into Lykkens for a broom, a lamp chimney, a leather halter. An Ace comb, a hair net, a corset, a tin of lice powder. A pair of shoes, a cotton frock, a yard of gingham, a card of red glass buttons. Years later, after he was well started in the community, Carl stocked his shelves with shorts, a form of leisure wear that the village defined as its own special invention, although it's debatable how much work went into thinking them up; they were simply cheap cotton trousers with the legs chopped off.

Resorts sometimes served as laboratories for experiments in new forms of social dress, and believe me those shorts stood out. It was impossible not to see them coming, the old guys in shorts, the bald knobby knees, the fuzzy white shins, the black socks sagging down to the sandaled feet. For good measure, Carl had a manufacturer in Los Angeles make up a supply of shorts in assorted colors.

> They came and my goodness they just went like hot cakes. It got to the point where I had to order up to 18s and 20s . . . the old gals, they liked them too. Tony Burke got busy then and photographed some of the pretty girls in shorts and sent them to *Physical Culture* . . . which was quite a popular magazine in those days. Soon they were getting shorts all over the country. Some cities barred them. I had a contingent from the church come in one day and ask me to desist selling shorts because, they said, I was ruining the morals of the young people.

Carl Lykken, corrupter of youth, seasoned retailer, telephone operator, Western Union messenger, and village postmaster under Wilson, Harding, and Coolridge ("I couldn't *give* that job away"). It was also Carl's patriotic duty to handle COD packages: COD chicks, COD reptiles, COD limburger cheese ("Boy, did that stink up the store . . . we thought it was a dead mouse"). An even worse shipment, if such can be imagined, was the meat that Otto Adler would order regularly for his Red Front Hotel and just as regularly be too broke to bail out. Beef did not keep long in Lykkens Store, in those good old days—were they really!—when an ice box was basically a box of ice. The ice arrived by freight from Banning, in three-hundred-pound blocks wrapped in heavy blankets. The blocks would melt to a hundred pounds en route, then melt some more in the store, getting smaller and smaller by half again. So before long, Adler's beef would decompose (turn prime was the popular expression), at which point it was buried "with a minimum display of grief and no Biblical reference."

Equally basic was the air conditioner: a wet gunnysack with a fan whose blades battered the hot air around, keeping the bills and invoices in a state of perpetual flutter. Fortunately, what little tourist season there was trickled to an end in April and dried up completely in May. With the long, insufferable summer coming on, when any movement—putting on clothes, preparing meals—became a campaign, exit was everyone's priority. It sounds so dismal, the village in June, a stricken land populated by a handful of moth-eaten coyotes and their human counterparts, the sorry few who hadn't the means to leave. How they must have suffered, those people. I see them in their underwear, collapsed on their cots, their heads lurched to one side, their eyes rolled shut, as if they'd been gunned down. August drives them to drink (so go the rumors) and to otherwise lose themselves until October, at which time they meet to see who has survived.

Several decades passed before the village enjoyed commercial air conditioning of the evaporative kind. But perhaps *enjoyed* isn't the right word. We had one, a huge water-fed thing that blew like mad and smelled slightly of fish (they were not called swamp coolers without reason). Movie theaters offered the first refrigerated air conditioning. How well I remember the posters for coming attractions plastered with ersatz icicles and signs promising "20 Degrees Cooler Inside." Not long after that, modern air conditioners began rolling off conveyor belts and into just about every home in the desert. But by then the golden years had become more than a little dulled.

* * *

Talk about those golden years long enough and eventually the Amado Street School comes up, a tidy white clapboard that speaks of Palm Springs like no place else. Here in the cramped space of one room, the various social strata of the village came together in one institution, the dark-haired Cahuillas and the corn-silk blonds, each kid called upon, turn by turn, to recite to a harried country-mouse teacher. Throughout the lessons a great potbelly stove roared and crackled, guzzling whatever driftwood could be scrounged in the bed of the Whitewater, a river dry much of its length, much of the year. Behind the stove, a commode held a large basin for washing up, a dish of lye soap, and an earthen crock filled with lemonade to keep the kids cool, or at least cooler, when the spring sun beat through the big windows. You can fill in the rest yourself, the wooden floor swept clean every evening, the flag furled neatly on its pole, the portraits of grim-lipped American presidents framed in ornate gilt. Anything more would have been wildly beyond the community's resources.

The world outside the classroom contained two privies, and a playground that was nothing more than a patch of desert encircled by a fence, beyond which the rattlesnakes lay waiting, coil upon coil, defying a kid to shuffle a barefoot step closer. Here, along with the usual monkey business of recess, I imagine much time was spent gazing toward the cool depths of Tahquitz Canyon. Because at three o'clock, everyone broke for the door, grabbed fishing poles, and disappeared with a surprising suddenness.

Ah! the old Tahquitz Canyon of my own misspent youth, a haven sublimely free from the dreary problems posed in algebra books. On a day fragrant with spring, a bunch of us would tell our moms we were going to school; then we'd hike off instead to the canyon (it felt like a jailbreak, and of course we suffered punishment the next day). Everywhere the terrain was rugged, the talus treacherous. Tahquitz Falls shook the boulders beneath our feet as we took flying leaps into the trout pools. We swam. We floated. We stretched out on our backs in the bright gap of sunlight, wreaths of cigarette smoke surrounding us, as carefree as kids can be. But it was a false comfort, and I always felt slightly anxious in that canyon. Not because of the cigarettes, swiped from a mother's purse, but because the canyon itself was dangerous. Every year incautious hikers disappeared up there beyond the first falls; our mothers would read to us from the newspaper. The police would call out Jim Maynard, a folk hero in my memory of him, a husky red-faced man whose strength was the strength of ten and whose skill was in finding lost hikers. Big Jim was so accustomed to finding them, or more often their broken bodies, most of the time he knew exactly where to look. Dead kids haunted that canyon to scare the living into obedience.

The Amado Street School went through twenty teachers in as many years, and I doubt that any of their contemporaries would envy the small niche they made in history. They were viewed as missionaries who took learning to those anxious to receive, and their social and professional lives, by today's standards, were bound by rules and incredibly boring.

One of the maverick teachers our desert seemed to breed was Edmund Jaeger, a solitary man who tucked himself away in a shanty at the mouth of Tahquitz Canyon. Born in Nebraska, Jaeger entered Palm Springs history in 1914. He had just completed a journey through the mountains, a thousand-mile expedition on foot that left him with a minor injury and a major need for employment. By happy coincidence, the

Amado Street School needed a teacher, a position that usually went begging. Jaeger was hired on the spot, but with the understanding that the average daily attendance wouldn't drop below five students, in which case, the school would lose county and state support. Hence, Jaeger occasionally found it necessary to borrow one or two kids from the lone homesteaders at Seven Palms, a couple who were disinclined to let a year pass without adding a new baby to their brood.

In all respects Jaeger was a teacher to his fingertips, a font of biological information. We have all seen this man, walking up and down the classroom, hands clasped behind his back, talking earnestly about the desert's creatures, disclosing the secrets of their private lives, as if they lived with him in his shanty, which, of course, many of them did. His lessons were lively, his props catch-as-catch-can: *Good morning, class. We're going to have a little anatomy lesson on this, ah, lab specimen.* By a stroke of luck, on his way to school one morning, Jaeger had stumbled upon a coyote, grinning horribly but otherwise quite dead; a good teacher had to make the most of whatever came to hand. After he had exhausted all manner of exterior information on the coyote, the kids, being kids, then wanted to see what lurked inside. For such an intelligent man, Jaeger didn't think very well. Without missing a beat, he reached into his pocket, extracted a pocketknife, and went to work parting the fur, slitting the skin, laying aside the muscles, tracing the nerves. One by one he identified the organs, turning them over in their dull, various colors. That's the heart. That's the liver. Those are the kidneys.

Now the kids knew all about coyotes, and something quite intimate about themselves as well (they knew they weren't supposed to be interested in such things, so they had never asked their mothers). A girl in blond pigtails, Ellen Maxwell, took it all with grave attention. "He showed us how we looked inside," she logged into her diary. "We all thought we were solid through and through and were terribly surprised." Here then was the lesson of a lifetime, or at least one that stayed with the kids all afternoon. Indeed there was a world of talk in those kitchens, and I cannot tell you how displeased the mothers were. Mr. Jaeger did *what*? Surely not. Oh the shame of it! With a collective energy, they marched on the school to have it out with Mr. Jaeger, to make him understand their horror. No sir, no more coyotes! No more anatomy lessons! I don't want my children to know what I'm like inside, one mother explained. Which of course was the end of that.

After his understandably brief teaching career at the Amado Street School, Edmund Jaeger dropped out to resume his own education at Occidental College. After earning his degree, he stepped up the career ladder to become head of the zoology department at Riverside College (beyond that, he discovered the hibernating poorwill, hailed by ornithologists as one of the most significant discoveries of its kind). But Jaeger was never a chair polisher, as they called them. He was a genuine scientist with real interests outside himself and the concerns for salary, position, and success. When he was not in the field collecting specimens—of which more than four hundred landed in the Smithsonian Institute—he was bent over his desk writing books, most of which are considered reference classics today. With a passion as pure as John Muir's, Jaeger presents us with chapters on such subjects as "Don Coyote," "The Poorwill's Secret Revealed," and "Eleodes, the Beetle That Stands on His Head." When you think of "Billy Bob-

Tail," with the lustrous black eyes set like "enormous hemispheres" on the all-knowing face, you think of that gentle-faced woodrat whose antics were all it took to activate Jaeger's tireless pen. The woodrat is a unique desert creature, and Jaeger wrote in response to that uniqueness:

> At one end of my poorly floored shanty is a knot-hole in the floor, to which Billy Bob-Tail has laid claim as his door to the mysterious, dark storehouse of his beneath the house. There were a good many grapefruit peels (Billy liked the bitter things) which were so very large that they would not go easily through the hole. Sometimes, when the clever wood rat could not get them down by pushing, he would sit on his haunches, take the peel in his paws, and nibble around the edges until it was small enough.

One rainy morning, as Jaeger lay on his cot watching, Billy tried to stuff an extra large orange peel down the hole to his storehouse underneath.

> It would not go down, in spite of his repeated attempts. Billy stopped and pondered. A sudden thought came to him. He dropped his peel beside the hole, went down the hole himself, pushed his head up through it, seized the orange peel, and pulled it through. This was invention, the product of reason, imagination, and judgement—and Billy a wood rat too.

Even more surprising was the help that Billy came to accept from Jaeger, "the many, many times I have pushed while he pulled. Here was the acceptance of cooperation, a trait befitting human beings."

* * *

In Jaeger's days at the Amado Street School, the way it worked was that you moved from grade to grade simply by moving from desk to desk, east to west, until you graduated. Then matters became complicated, as they were bound to. Because for a high school education you were sent to Banning. Off you'd go early in the morning, two hours on a bad road in a rusty country bus, thick black smoke billowing from the tailpipe. That is, if the engine started and if the road was open. Either you got home late or you didn't get home at all, if the weather was bad or if the bus broke down, as it did more often than not, partly because of age and partly because the engine was strained far beyond its limits. Should you miss the bus because of after-school activities, you then had to wait at the service station on the corner, a routine, like high school itself, that was interesting at first, then frustrating, then just plain boring. Nevertheless, it ultimately got you home. It was automatic. Anyone driving to Palm Springs in the evening would look for you at that station, smiling like an angel, your thumb stuck way out.

I came to know these kids of the Amado Street School, at least by reputation, the afternoon I was left to my own devices in the storage room of the Palm Springs Historical Society. What you would find within those old adobe walls, if you ever do find it among toppling piles of unfinished projects, among middens of dusty magazines, photo albums, and telephone books, among a rummage-sale assortment of old clothes, furniture, utensils, keepsakes, and other oddments that have somehow survived who knows how many domestic rearrangements, family moves, marriages, and deaths . . . that is, what you would find in that room is a wealth of primary source material, a bulk that threatens to separate you from the point of it all. Crunching crickets underfoot, one or two of which showed a twitch of slow-dying life, I moved down the aisles, carefully, for fear of triggering a paper slide. From industrial metal shelves bent under stacks of cardboard boxes bursting at the seams with fat sheaves of old letters and telegrams bound in twine, with invoices and press clippings bound by rubber bands that had melted in spots . . . that is, from a shelf I pulled down a cardboard box labeled School in big black letters. Warily I sat down at a desk (teaming, I felt sure, with hidden activity) and began burrowing through treasures that had been gathering dust since they were donated by the teachers. I studied layers of lined paper and cracked end-of-term photos, trying to match up the faces of the kids with Miss Newberry's careful longhand descriptions.

Here was Albert Gauff, born in Texas, a kid with a smile "that wouldn't come off." I see him in the schoolyard, hanging off the bottom of a galloping burro, plinking tin cans with a slingshot.

Here was Junior Omlin, all knuckles and knees. His perfect attendance record was ruined the day he was "stabbed by Brutus and carried off in a wheelbarrow."

Here was Junior Davis, a grinning freckle-face with a haystack of red hair and oversized ears that might have given him trouble in a strong wind. Born in Washington, he was "a hundred percent American boy" who would have kept Miss Newberry busy sanding away the obscenities carved into his desk.

In the box I also found a dog-eared primer entitled *Begin-*

163

ners' Book in Language, which aimed to give constructive answers to questions posed in the preface:

How shall we banish timidity among the children?

How shall we inoculate them against common errors in English?

Beginners' Book answered with exercises: how to write letters, how to write stories, how to use *ring, rang*; *drink, drank*; *see, saw*. Some of the lessons were laid out with stage-directions and props:

Chapter V . . . Have children bring pictures of wild animals, trick riders, circus parades. It would be the best of good luck if a large circus poster could be obtained and fastened on the front wall.

Chapter IX . . . Decorate room with Indian subject matter. A small Indian teepee may be pitched in one corner. A Navajo rug may adorn the wall. Have pupils draw tomahawks, Indian chiefs, squaws, and papooses on paper with colored crayons. The following are war whoops: Ki-yi, whoo-oo! Ki-yi, ki-yi, ki-yi, whoo-oo!

A better teaching aid took the form of the printing press that launched the village's first newspaper. I leafed through several issues of the *Desert Star*, so bold and innocent:

Rin-Tin-Tin and his trainer came to entertain us on Play Day. The trainer showed us how to teach our dogs tricks. Then he had the dog do these tricks. Rin-Tin-Tin did some of the acts for us that he has learned to do for the movies.

Jimmy Flynn brought a little humming bird's nest to class. The nest is on an oleander branch that forks. It is made of cobwebs, soap chips, oatmeal and grass. It is lined with feathers to make it soft. It is a very tiny nest.

One day last week an old man came to visit our room. He talked to us about Abraham Lincoln. He gave a prize to the one who was the quietest while he talked. Jessie won the prize.

I read bright little verses that celebrated such sentimental subjects as "Our Cactus Garden," "Christmas on the Desert," and "My Rabbit." I read that many children had gained weight since they started drinking milk at school. I learned from Dr. Kellogg of Battle Creek that if we eat the right kind of food, especially cornflakes, and leave tobacco and strong drink alone, we will live long and well. Copies of the *Desert Star*, each issue worried into shape between classes, would have been handed out while the pages were still cool and moist. The alcoholic vapor of the print had a thick fragrance that would be remembered long after the effects of the printed matter had worn off.

Will Rogers Jr. got his name on the school's enrollment when his famous father vacationed at the Desert Inn. Although inaccuracies can come with years of retelling, his teacher Katherine Finchy claimed that Will's schoolyard acrobatics formed the nucleus of our famous Desert Circus—an annual week-long event, during which time a pleasant sort of madness seeped through the village, growing ever more apparent with the weekend windup, when almost anything could happen, and usually did. The idea was for everyone to have fun.

The Desert Circus was far from being the kind of circus you ran away to join. Over the years, it had been hobbled into a parade, a beef cookout, a polo match with burros, a horse race with few rules and heavy betting, a Big Top Ball, a dance hall hilarity where respectable villagers did silly things, and a kangaroo court complete with a judge who tried and fined the unsuspecting, on any old charge, for no good reason except for the fun of it. The Desert Circus was started in 1934 and went on for so many years that parts of it, like the mounted posses, seemed to happen of their own accord. Then in 1981, for one reason or other, the old stalwart volunteers stopped participating, and the whole system, if system there ever was, broke down. But it was a joy while it lasted and is still a joy to remember, even as old sentimentalists like me brood over its disappearance.

As a child I grew into the Desert Circus as it grew, participating in it more times than I can remember. The parade was divided in two. One half of the village was in it and the other half watched it, assembled variously on benches, curbing, and lawn chairs, the more adventurous on the rooftops of shops. There was a glorious expectancy in waiting for the start, which was always delayed for fifteen minutes due to technical problems that were never announced. We would stretch our necks and strain our eyes, then a slight flutter in the stomach, and down the street it came: the marching bands in tunics trimmed in silver and gold, the *oompah-pah* carrying over the empty desert, the Stars and Stripes flapping loyally in the breeze; the sequined majorettes with their bouncing ponytails, tossing batons higher than the rooftops; the Indian chiefs, the unicyclists, the knot of jugglers, the tumble of acrobats; the troupe of men in bowler hats and baggy pants, clowning around, squirting plastic flowers. Here were the nubile beauties draped over freshly washed Cadillacs, patting their hairdos, fluttering their eyelashes, looking as pretty as they knew how. Here were the little kids, their pet goats tied up in red bows; and the world famous poodles in their ballerina skirts and funny hats, walking stiffly and unnaturally on hind legs, doing tricks for biscuits. Here were the equestrians in their century-old spurs and tailored finery, as if this were yet the age of the caballeros, when those who had money wore a good share of it on the saddles of their blooded mounts. Here was Mazumbo the elephant, fanning its ears, swinging its trunk to a private tempo, Mother Coffman perched on its big hairy back, the two of them overwhelming everything in sight. Here was all of Hollywood: Bob Hope, Hopalong Cassidy, Gene Autry, Chuck Conners, Kirk Douglas, William Holden, Red Skelton, Dean Martin, Jimmy Durante, Frank Sinatra, Trini Lopez, Edgar Bergen and Charlie McCarthy . . . so many celebrities over the years, we stopped gasping at their presence.

Yes sir, for us lucky enough to have grown up in Palm Springs, the Desert Circus was a big deal, a very big deal. But I don't mean to suggest that it started out in a big way. In 1935 Jacob Upstitch found it somewhat lacking. "I am an acrobat," he informed the editor of the *Palm Springs Limelight*,

and have good clown suit. I feel I would be a knockout addition to the Desert Circus and will without any doubts wow them but must have fifty dollars first. If you will forward that amount to me I will make your parade a success no matter how bad it looks at this date. I am used to carrying the WHOLE show at very select social gatherings and never get nervous no matter how many things go wrong. Believe me I have had a lot of experience and am always a scream wherever I go. I have a universal appeal as women follow me around and I can tell by their faces that I am clicking with them at all times. I am no Pansy and men respect my act. My wife is a midget and you can have her too if you want her only she's not comical like I am.

P.S. I could shave the price a little bit. I have false whiskers also.

* * *

Ten gongs ring out above VillageFest, signaling the end of my research for tonight. The awnings come down and the crowd thins to a trickle. The farmers load up their empty crates and roll their old pickups back to the farms. The increasingly out-of-tune musicians ease their instruments back into velvet-lined cases and race off to play at Venice Beach. All in all, nothing special went on here. It just felt like a village event ought to feel. And sometimes it's just nice to find a place where people are friendly and the food is good. Palm Springs has done itself proud.

FIVE

A Week without Walls

A nudist camp for the San Jacinto Mountains is planned. However lest there be a regular exodus from here, it is well to announce beforehand that the camp will be guarded by savage German shepherd dogs. Evidently, the canines will respect the persons regularly enrolled. Those attending must bring their own bedding and nothing is said about clothes but that the land is "free from reptiles and insects."

—THE DESERT SUN 1936

*S*UNSHINE VILLAS, that's one world. The San Jacinto Mountains, that's another. How often I have sat with my morning coffee, watching that wall of granite, tinged with purple, violet, pink, the colors flaring, the sun rising fast. Whatever pleasure I take from wild nature began for me up there, and even today, whenever I feel a desperate need for solitude, I haul my desert soul to that remembered paradise.

The mountain Saint Hyacinth, the *sierra San Jacinto*, pronounced Ha-*seen*-toe, not *jack*-in-toe. It stands at the northern end of the Peninsular Range, an 800-mile backbone running the length of Baja California. From my distance here beside the pool, I see no foothills anywhere, no gentle swells, no gradual ascents, no curves. But if I keep my eye on that mountain long enough, I'll see a marvel of faces and figures sculpted by gulch and ravine, sunlight and shadow: The Angel. The Abraham Lincoln. The Madonna and Child. The Witch of Tahquitz Canyon, there in her stovepipe hat, cruising on her witchy broom, plain as day, an awesome sight.

My thoughts seem always to be somewhere on that mountain. Ever since I can remember, it has been my ambition to walk its length, and even now such a project flames my imagination. The mileage isn't so great: thirty-five miles from end to end, nothing that would require an air drop of food. In one of those moments of insane optimism, I see myself starting, say, in Snow Creek Canyon, a section of the Pacific Crest Trail that looks extremely difficult to climb. I'd hike along the ridge for a few days to Highway 74, then down the Palm Canyon trail to Hermits Bench, where I'd take a chance on catching a lift home. To be true to such moments is the challenge, and I am deeply disappointed in myself for letting it pass. It's so much easier to skip it, to just say that the legs are no longer strong, the knees no longer flexible, the feet no longer willing to take instruction. What I'd like is to have already done the trip, to have it on my record as a feat accomplished.

On the other hand, when dailiness becomes too much for me, my alternative to Sunshine Villas (and most Sunshine Villagers do need one) is to escape for a week of backcountry camping via the Palm Springs Aerial Tramway. "You're going *alone*? Is that safe?" My mother wants assurance, although on this July morning, on these respectable, elderly streets, her fears seem unreasonable.

"Yes, I think so. Pretty safe," I say assuredly, although on any given month someone is likely to die up there, from hypothermia, exhaustion, and trauma, from a heart attack or a fall, accidental or not—there are plenty of scenic overlooks to leap from. Bears, rattlesnakes, and mountain lions are further cause for alarm. So are ground squirrels, for here is your reserve of bubonic plague, one flea-hop from host to hiker. Unfriendly strains of *E. coli* are another big worry. Say a wandering deer releases a few billion of these organisms into the creek. You dip your Sierra cup miles down stream and inadvertently swallow several of the little buggers, who then set off on a leisurely trip to your gut, where they will double their numbers every twenty minutes or so. After a few days you start to feel bad, as if the rest of your trip might not proceed according to plan. Then the feared moment comes. Down you go in the throes of dysentery, in a hellish wash of pain. You hug your ribs and groan beastly groans. You thrash around and call for your mother, oh *please*, oh *please*, oh *please*. You pull leaves over yourself, pine needles, dirt. Done for, you think. Barely conscious, senseless day and night, you lose all desire to get up. Then comes shock, organ failure, and finally, charitably, death. You can only hope that you are sufficiently coherent to record every agonizing step in your notebook.

"Take your pepper spray." My mother's voice in my ear, a couple of final words, no more. Having gained the wisdom of age and experience, she knows the futility of protest and thus avoids putting a strain on family relations. In this household where the old and the older take care of each other, the secret to getting along is to underplay our mother-daughter roles.

* * *

You can't just go backpacking, you have to pack, which is an adventure in itself. Ultimately, of course, to survive in the wilds only three things really matter: water, shelter, and food.

Imagine John Muir in the Sierras, drinking from a creek, making his bed a hollow tree and his dinner a crust of bread. Not so spartan was Charles Francis Saunders, Muir's counterpart in the San Jacintos. Saunders was wont to pack around a canteen, a blanket, a skillet, and all the "et cetera" that *he* required for survival. Even after eighty years his advise is still fresh:

> By careful selection and the exercise of self-denial, a temperate eater can keep the weight of a week's comestibles down to fifteen pounds or so . . . For instance, one package two-minute oat-food; one package seedless raisins; one can choclat-achor (a powdered instant chocolate made from the whole bean); two small cans salmon; one can powdered milk; two pounds dried apricots, peaches, or prunes; one pound English walnuts (hulled); one pound cheese; one package egg noodles, rice, or cornmeal; four small cans beans; a pound or two of hard crackers (a multi-grain sort called Grant's is excellent); a tin of tea; sugar; salt. If the German meal sausages of prewar days come again, let some of them be included . . . Of course, if you are clever enough to catch trout as you travel, your pack may be correspondingly reduced and your fare enlivened.

And again:

> In the wildest and most remote haunts of Nature, a woman . . . rarely has need for any heavier shoes than the average stout walking boot, nor for a skirt above the ankles . . . Soft colors that will not frighten the birds and small animals about camp, will add to their comfort and your own pleasure; and plainly made linen-colored waists with pretty collars, will be found welcome . . . It may be

said, in passing, that the wearer of clothes reasonably clean and neat and devoid of freakishness, combined with a generous supply of baggage, will cause you invariably to be set down as a tenderfoot.

Today's wilderness traveler, if well organized, can go into the San Jacintos infinitely better supplied than Saunders (not to mention Muir). Lightweight gear allows me to be my own pack mule. Think of it! The world does not only get worse.

Long list in hand, I stare at the mountain of gear piled on the floor of my bedroom. I can't just shovel it in any old way. I have to be organized. First off, into the main load-bearing sack of my Kelty go the knapsack, the water purifier, and the comestibles, each meal zipped inside a plastic bag, and of exactly the right proportion (and constantly unzipped, readjusted, and rezipped throughout the trip). A dozen rye crackers, a chunk of mozzarella cheese, two tins of sardines, and a durable but unappealing summer sausage, shot with chemicals and overharsh on the stomach juices—this will be my diet for a week. It's a monotony barely interrupted by nuts, dried fruit, and something the health food store across the street calls a nutrition bar, a conglomerate of whey protein and raisin paste, with a touch of soy for taste. I get pretty sick of it all, but down it goes to the last crumb.

In go the binoculars and field guides, the camera and lenses, the wool sweater full of moth holes, and as many socks as I can cram into the crannies. Into the side pockets go all the et cetera that *I* require for survival: eyebrow pencil, mirror, dental floss (also handy for emergency sutures), pack of Sominex (even under the best of conditions I am a light and anxious sleeper). Into the map pocket go the USGS topographic maps

(I pretend I know how to read them) and the latest *Back-packer*-approved compass (I mean to learn how to use it some day, although if I did I'm sure I'd be shocked at where the needle wants to point). OK, what else? Water bottles. Check. Toilet paper. Check. A book, any of the good works as long as it's a paperback and I can make it dirty with an easy conscious. In goes the rain jacket, although I won't be needing it according to the weatherman. It hardly matters that Hurricane Bonnie is wrecking a few Bahamas and Tropical Storm Charley is romping through Mexico, the Coachella Valley is having no weather at all thanks to a ridge of high pressure bulging fatly over the Southwest. That's to be expected. We aren't supposed to get rain in July. It just about can't rain unless a monsoon slips in from Arizona.

Into a small nylon sack goes the sleeping bag. Into another sack goes the air mattress, an ingenious invention by which I will sleep on my own hot breath. And into yet another sack goes the one-person, three-season tent I bought when I decided to become a solo traveler. During the dinner hour, when the breeze dies and the whining insects rise from the meadow, I eat in there, flat on my back, listening to the *tick*, *tick*, *tick* of tiny bodies pelting the red slope of ceiling a foot above my head, the crackers, cheese, and tin of sardines balanced unsteadily on my chest, rising and settling with my every breath.

Which is to say that I get no pleasure from backpacking, from pitching a tent, crawling through the porthole entrance, arranging everything inside; from sleeping on the ground, cocooned in synthetic fibers, cold and otherwise uncomfortable, never sleeping deeply but lying there beneath the surface of consciousness, listening to the scurries of nocturnal rodentia inches from my head. I do not awaken each morning with the certainty that, yes sir! this is the life for me. Backpacking is a great discomfort to which I adjust only slowly, but it's the only way to get beyond the reach of roads.

So. Strap the stuff-sacks to the pack frame, snug everything tight, hope the buckles hold. Fully-loaded, my backpack always seems intolerably heavy until it's on my back. At which point, the brilliantly designed strapping, webbing, and cushioning so balances the load, I forget (on rare occasions) that it's there. Heaving it onto the bathroom scale, I find that it weighs forty-two pounds, ten pounds too much for a frame my size to carry, according to all the books I have read. In the interest of saving weight—not to mention fuss and bother—I have already eliminated the stove and fuel canisters. Now I return *Western Reptiles and Amphibians* to the bookshelf. I unpack the long camera lens, three rolls of film, and the ground cloth for the tent. Going to ridiculous lengths, I break my mirror in half and saw the handle off my toothbrush (I'll simply comb my hair with my fingers). Now the pack weighs thirty-six pounds, still too much, but it will have to do. I check the list, check it again. Ready, set, go.

"Have a good time. Don't get lost." My mother, ensconced in cushiony comfort, is perfectly happy to be going nowhere. I'll leave her in the company of CNBC's stock market analyst, the blinds drawn, the a/c jacked to the max. In my mother's universe, it's seventy-eight degrees, summer and winter.

"I will. I won't."

* * *

Ten minutes from Sunshine Villas, curve by treacherous curve, my taxi climbs the grade to Tramwayland, a task to which my

175

micropowered Volkswagen was unequal. Ultimately, of course, old vans are best off in the hands of people with money to burn. I say this after AAA had to rescue me three times in as many months, towing me to a tumble-down junkyard, its painted name faded into antique. Even so, its owner, Mike, came through for me every time, for a minimal fortune. And every time he would turn to me and say in a worrisomely eager way, "You have *no idea* how lucky you are. *No idea.*" Which meant that my van bore all the signs of impending collapse, and that if I kept going on an engine that fired on less than four uncertain cylinders, the next mile could be my last. Should the engine give up entirely, the chance of a normal person stopping in the dark, on a lonely stretch of highway, was not good.

Of course, bandits are found downvalley, too. Not knowing what to do, yet compelled by anxiety to do *something*, I sold the van and pocketed what you might expect from an auto mart called Cash For Cars. Beyond that, I have not suffered in the least. Palm Springs is still small enough—and safe enough in daylight—to go about one's business on bicycle or on foot, and a surprising number of people do so. As for myself, I have bought the necessary groceries and returned home intact, my purchases protruding from voluminous nylon panniers slung over the back wheel of my mountain bike. I have had haircuts, mailed packages, and kept dental appointments. I have attended potlucks and regular meetings of the Writers, the Hikers, the Seniors, and the Pioneers. In the unlikely event I should seek further adventure, I can belt myself into an Alaskan Airliner and be held captive for a number of long hours, stiff and slightly anxious. The alternative—traveling by train—promises even greater adventure. I see myself climbing

aboard—incredibly—at 3:15 in the morning, at what is eu-
phemistically described as the Palm Springs Station, as if an
unsheltered platform tucked between the sand dunes could be
called a station. *What's it doing way out here?* you think.

We are off to a bad start, Joe, my taxi-driver, and I. How he
managed to avoid a large snake suddenly in front of us is a
mystery, but there it was, and it didn't seem to faze him. After
my initial apprehension, the ride becomes even more troubling as our steady progress up the grade becomes a slow
progress up the grade. We're doing forty, doing thirty-five,
doing thirty, the automatic transmission protesting, the radia-
tor about to burst. After a first fool urge to caution Joe—hey,
look at your temperature gauge!—I abandon myself to fate.
Two thousand feet higher, he drops me in front of the valley
station. He should have dropped me half a mile back by the
looks of things. His engine is blowing steam. A pool of coolant
is spreading underneath. I am somehow embarrassed about
this, as if the fault were mine. "No problem," Joe says matter-
of-factly as he helps me calculate the fare, plus tip, less senior's
discount. "No problem," he repeats. "Happens all the time."
Standing beside the trunk, he holds up my loaded pack as if it
weighs nothing. I back into the proffered straps, like a mule
between shafts, and lever the pack heroically onto my back.

Inside the valley station I line up behind a busload of jolly
greyhairs, all talking amiably to each other and fanning themselves with postcards. The name tags (Hi! Wilma Morris—
Cedar Rapids) suggest a packaged tour. At the counter I buy a
senior's ticket, push through the turnstile, and take my place
beside Muriel Coombs (Wichita). Thus corralled in the waiting room amid high-pitched chatter and good-natured jock-
eying for space, I have nothing to do but wait for perhaps five

minutes. On the chance I might see something new, I focus my attention on the view out the oversized windows, a craggy geology of such appalling dimensions it belittles the toy tram. The cable car—cunningly contrived to revolve as it climbs—is immobile for the moment, suspended in space so it seems that one good gust of wind would carry it away. Its bright gold paint contrasts with the gray granite of the mountain; the idea is to make the wreckage easier to spot. To move up the cables from which the cable car hangs, that is, to move two and a half miles up the face of the sheerest mountain in the country, is to move among five zones of climate. If one of those cables were to break, so would a lot of other things, in extremely rapid and disastrous succession. Which brings me to the towers from which the cables hang, and how precariously they cling to their granite outcroppings, so finely balanced there a fingertip might send them crashing down. At this point, Muriel Coombs turns to the window and furrows her brow, as if wondering whether I see anything wrong anywhere, and hoping that in case I do, I will have the good sense to mention it.

Ticketed and cleared for boarding, we put our trust in the capable hands of the attendant, who packs us in like sardines. By dint of miracle, we take to the air, while a recorded voice describes dramatically the engineering marvels that pull us along. To get rid of a few statistics: The vertical ascent is 5,873 feet, that is from 2,643 feet at the valley station to 8,516 feet at the mountain station. The weight of the eleven cables totals 330 tons; the weight of steel in the five towers totals 263 tons. The tallest tower is 226 feet high. To someone, somewhere, these figures may have meaning. They don't to me. They are grindingly dull. They threaten to contaminate the thrill of the ride, which I assure you is very real.

* * *

The idea for the Palm Springs Aerial Tramway was born in 1926, when the great powers of the Southern Pacific Railroad envisioned their passengers throwing snowballs at each other every season of the year. Except that nothing came of the idea until 1936, when Francis Crocker, then district manager of the electric company, took it on with fanatical devotion. Seeking support for the project, he approached the local merchants and press. Funds were raised. The terrain was surveyed. The mountain was climbed on horseback. Trips were made to Switzerland and Austria to study aerial trams in the Alps. Plans were submitted. Land use permits were received. A bill was presented, voted down, presented again, voted down, presented again . . . the process being awash with government regulations and further complicated by endlessly interfering environmentalists. In a temporary victory for common sense, plans were squashed for roads, hotels, lodges, an ice skating rink, a ski lift, ski runs—as if it were sensible to cut down swaths of timber on a mountain that receives so little snowfall it's measured in skimpy inches on the best of years. Finally, somehow, the bill slipped through. Crocker was victorious, he was triumphant, he was declared Father of the Palm Springs Aerial Tramway, the world renowned Palm Springs Aerial Tramway, like the pyramids of Egypt, the Hanging Gardens of Babylon, the Colossus of Rhodes.

Whatever your attitude, you cannot fail to be impressed by this monumental undertaking; few projects can compare. Because the terrain is so rugged, five Bell G-3 helicopters were used to transport crews and materials up the mountain. Prefab buildings and bulldozers, broken down in sections and whisked aloft in slings, were inched fastidiously down between the trees in Long Valley, the throb of rotors shattering the mountain hush. In every sense, the project called for audacity and a sense of adventure. So credit the pilots with completing it in two years (and 22,000 helicopter flights) with no loss of life. Now a mountaintop accessible only to mountaineers was suddenly within reach of millions, as near as a thought.

September 1963: "Tramway Dedicated," announced the headlines. It was a gray day in Palm Springs, the mountain engulfed in a drizzly gloom. All the same, the event went as expected. In a gust of high spirits, members of the Marine Corps Band flung themselves into a march, the tubas and trumpets blaring a celebratory sendoff against the mountain. Amid a storm of flashbulbs, reporters scurried around, trying to find out who was who among a galaxy of aging stars, most of whom were living off autographs and banquet appearances. Then everyone's attention settled on Edmund G. Brown as he showered gubernatorial blessings all over the event. Finally, with all the gravity appropriate to her role, Bernice Brown shot the cork off a bottle of champagne and after two swipes broke it over the cable car, for which she was generously applauded.

That day somebody had the ride of his life ("Brown Grips Steel Railing, Wishes It Were Disneyland"). Even after countless trips, it's still like that for me, this barely controlled terror. The attendant slams the door shut on a full complement of strangers, all of whom suddenly find themselves in forced intimacy. Never has a door been so locked as that steel slab. With an awful lurch, the car launches itself, and with a minimum of human interference, hauls its giddy way up the narrow crack of Chino Canyon, past slabs of sheer uncompromising granite, past outcrops that fall away in fans of fractured scree, past pine trees that list at crazy angles—in places it looks like the whole mountain is coming right at you. At each tower, the car swings more than it climbs, tipping you backward and forward, wearing out the cables even more than they already are. Then suddenly you're inside the clouds, a formless white void much like blindness or death. Some people whoop with joy as the minutes pass. Others stand rigid and still, their fists clenched white around the railing. It's easy to imagine what's going through their minds: *We're going too fast. We're going too high. We're too heavy to bring off this trick. We've tempted fate once too often. We're definitely goners.*

On the day of the inaugural run, the governor's car docked itself at the mountain station with nothing more dramatic than a bump (more than twelve million passengers have since shared the same good fortune). Although the rest of his long afternoon has not been preserved by the press, I think it can be roughly reconstructed. First the heroic feast, the tables banked with flowers, the courses coming and going by candlelight. Then the festive bottles of champagne, the crystal clinking all around. A second round splashes forth, a third, and by the time the bottles are drained, the tramway has been toasted so often it should last at least a thousand years.

Through the years Tramwayland has continued to give the local and distant press a succession of excitements, sometimes comic, sometimes tragic, but always unique. From a massive quarry of data, I offer a few chippings.

October 22, 1968. Tramway Animal Park opens. Petting zoo features Japanese silky chickens, Japanese deer, African pigmy goats, peacocks, and 20 white reindeer. Amphitheater features high wire act with South American macaws, piano duet by chimpanzee and monkey, and smart house cat opening a can of cat food. Dolphin tank to open in two weeks. Public invited to enter "Name the Dolphins" contest.

September 11, 1970. Tramway Animal Park closes. General Manager explains that running an animal compound in Chino Canyon is not practical.

December 3, 1976. Bobcat climbs power pole, fatally tangles with 33,000 volts, leaves 86 people stranded at mountain station. Washington visitor Orv Mauritzen reports:

> After the lights went out, they got a small emergency generator going. They told us that they could move the tram cars, but the ride would probably be very slow. It was the scariest ride of my life. We were barely moving and the car swung back and forth slowly. We had a lot of time to think about how far it was to the ground. And there were a number of elderly passengers whose legs soon gave out, so we had to huddle even closer to make room for them to sit. And one woman, with a heart condition, had forgotten her pills. Then a few people started getting sick, causing others to vomit. The ride was becoming a real nightmare. We sang every song we could think of.

Ninety minutes into the ordeal, the valley station comes into view, "a most welcome sight."

October 6, 1977. *Six Million Dollar Man* features tramway. Script calls for Lee Majors to walk along cables from highest tower to "stalled" tram car. Majors to perform his own stunts.

May 1, 1980. Two tramway employees break into control

room at valley station, fire up the tram, ride through pre-dawn dark to mountain station, break into vault, leave with over $3,000.

June 25, 1984. Bolt from shock absorber snaps, causing 30-pound chunk of metal to crash through Plexiglas roof of tram car. Ontario woman dies of massive head injuries. Three others hurt. Tram attendant radios for help while car and 45 passengers continue down mountain. Workers "saddened" by tramway's first accident.

July 10, 1995. Van overheats in parking lot of valley station, engine catches fire, fuel tank explodes. Flaming fuel flows across pavement, destroys two vehicles, damages five others. Owners return from mountain to find notes on their windshields.

March 22, 2000. Linda Sue Richard, 41, Victor Lee Bryan, 21, and Sky Vreeken, age unknown, carry on bizarre acts at mountain station. Diners watch as trio fling food and bottles off cliff, jump on dinner plates. Tram employees escort trio to tram car. During descent, 40 people, including children, watch Richard perform lewd act on Bryan. All three are cited for intoxication and littering. Bryan and Richard are arrested for lewd conduct. "We really are shocked," reports tramway's general manager.

What happened on July 31, 1991, was at once a major media event and a tragedy beyond the reach of words. As waves of panic and grief eddied outward across the telephone lines, reporters gave us the news in pages of headlines: "7 Die, 53 Hurt As Girl Scout Bus Overturns on Tramway Road" and "Parents Anxiously Await Life or Death Calls" and "Brakes Probed for Cause of Fatal Bus Crash." They gave us quotes from a tearful Mayor Sonny Bono: "Goddamn it, goddamn it, this is just so sad . . . This is the worst day ever in the history of the city . . . the worst disaster in Palm Springs." They gave us photographs, of the mangled school bus on its side at the bottom of a ravine; of the rescuers, still in shock, picking over the ghastly collage of twisted passenger seats, picnic coolers, tennis shoes, and athletic bags; of the long ominous lines of gurneys standing outside the emergency rooms at three area hospitals. And because it happened right here, it was almost as though we had all lost family.

* * *

Mercifully, my tram ride is short and without incident, a twelve-minute shot—the ears pop five times. The attendant hopes we have enjoyed our flight as he off-loads us into what should, by rights, be thin air. Suddenly it isn't summer anymore. I have arrived so fast that my shirt, still damp with sweat, chills me to the bone. I put on my heavy shirt and still I shiver.

Forgive me for expressing my humble opinion, but as architecture the mountain station is not beautiful. And yet it was apparently constructed without thought of expense. There it stands, a delirious fantasy of wood and glass mounted precariously on the very brink of the escarpment, maximizing the view at the risk of losing it all. The lofty three-level interior gives you that exalted feeling of being somewhere special, particularly the dining room, which is big enough to run several separate banquets comfortably at once. Here, in one corner, various mountain fauna have been put on stuffed display, their glass eyes staring astounded at the steaming buffet. The centerpiece is an endangered bighorn sheep, seized, most likely, from a rogue taxidermist. Although the ram is no longer looking his best, his stance, attitude, and slightly anxious face have been duplicated exactly. He's all the more convincing with two ground squirrels, very much alive, scampering around his hocks. What wildlings nest in the pots and pans, I can't tell you.

The glory of the mountain station is the view beyond the floor-to-ceiling windows. This is as far into the San Jacintos as most visitors ever get. After catching only a vague glimpse of the tall-timbered distance, they assemble at each vantage point and shoot spools of snapshots, sunglasses perched in their hair. Then they depart, the compulsory photo session being the point of the trip, not the means of remembering it. Back home, they will hand the pictures to their friends and tell them they've been to the San Jacintos, meaning that they rode the tram, bought coffee mugs in the gift shop, and ate a smoky mess of ribs on the breezy eastern terrace, which, I should warn you, is positioned so horribly high above the Coachella Valley that you feel grateful for the iron railing.

When you step out the western door of the mountain station, you are faced with a steep, winding descent on a cement ramp (it's heated in winter to melt the ice so that women in teetery stiletto heels can safely tiptoe a few steps into the wilderness and hurry back to the cocktail lounge without losing their good humor). Where the cement ends the trail through Long Valley begins. Long Valley, Tamarack Valley, Round Valley, Little Round Valley; the map-makers used no more imagination than that.

Long Valley is a picnic ground where families sit at tables among nests of sandwich wrappers and pop cans. Here you'll find a string of mules for hire, a series of short self-guided trails, and a rustic cabin with a ranger inside who issues permits for the backcountry and sees to it that a rescue is organized should you fail to be home on schedule. Actually, I have no schedule. My plans are a vague, agreeable dream. This, at least, is what I have in mind as I pocket my permit, tip my cap against the glare, and launch myself unprotected into the surroundings. My pack feels, gee, *heavier* somehow than I expected.

Lying in an oval basin below San Jacinto Peak, Round Valley (my destination) is but a small part of the San Jacinto backcountry, a wilderness managed by the good folks at two government agencies. The San Bernardino National Forest claims the San Jacinto Wilderness, and the state of California claims the adjacent Mount San Jacinto Wilderness State Park: separate zones, separate offices, separate wilderness permits, different rules, just to make things confusing. Yet to tag any of it *wilderness* seems like a fraud. It's the easiest backcountry to reach, the most visited, the most explored. What strikes you is the abundance of human beings and the absence of large predatory mammals, most of whom were exterminated during the rampaging days of the Old West, when every four-legged creature was naturally regarded as something to be eaten, ridden, poisoned, or trapped.

When ranchers raised cattle in these mountains, their ranches always attracted grizzlies. And grizzlies always meant trouble; we have that from the old journals. As the bears went about their business, searching for something to eat, they covered a lot of ground, their powerful legs taking them dozens of miles in one direction, then dozens of miles in another direction, all their lives. Too often they would blunder into a ranch, because it was impossible to travel dozens of miles without blundering into a ranch; the maps in my backpack are tagged clear across with the names of ranchers: Thomas, Garner, Reed, Wellman, Tripp, Spitler, Hamilton, Vandeventer—a valley here, a meadow there, a mountain top, a pass, a creek.

What stands out in the old journals is a misdirected rite known as "the party bear hunt." It goes something like this: A grizzly blunders into a ranch. A cowboy sets a trap, that is, he leads an old horse into a meadow, shoots it, then trails the entrails around to scent the bear. The next morning he rides to the ridge and looks down on the meadow and the bear asleep beside his half-eaten meal.

Suddenly, at the signal, a mad rush begins, a stampede of activity—cowboys, horses, and hounds. Down the mountainside they all go, startling the bear into action. The bear runs and runs, paws pounding the ground, big rear end wobbling. A rope catches him by the neck, bringing him up short. He bites the rope in two. More ropes catch him by the foreleg, the hind leg, the neck. The horses, trained to handle cattle, keep the ropes taut. The bear, biting ropes, raking horses, slapping dogs right and left, is yanked simultaneously in three directions. Now gagged and held, he staggers and falls, clearly losing strength. The guns come out. Bullets tear into the bear, no one bothering to take aim, just whanging away with both barrels. *Take that and that and that.* The bear lies where he falls, slowly dying in his own blood, chomping his big jaws at every last layer of rope. After a safe interval, someone walks over and kicks him, the reputation of a half-dead grizzly being what it is. Then the talk turns to measurements, everyone wanting to get into the newspapers.

There were a lot of grizzlies to go through back then, and the cowboys felt honor-bound to get every last one, to make every acre of mountain safe for cows. Consequently, the day came when so few bears remained they were named like pets. Old Three Toes, Old White Face, Old Phantom were whaling big bears that had grown exceedingly wary in the ways of men and dogs, having learned that the price of life lay in making their habitat on the brushiest hillsides and in changing location from time to time at the slightest hint of cowboy. But still the killing continued, until the California grizzly disappeared completely from California. But to write about wildlife anywhere these days is to write of the end of the world.

Nearly everyone who supports wilderness supports the idea of bears, so intimately are bears identified with wilderness. After the grizzlies were gone, it was still fairly easy to see black bears in the Sierras. Find a garbage dump and you find the bears. But whatever role wild nature decreed for wild bears, licking the inside of tin cans did not figure in. So in a program that would both rid the Sierras of campground bears and fill the ecological void left by the grizzlies, "surplus" blacks were transplanted to the San Bernardino Mountains. Or rather, they were introduced; black bears are not native to Southern California.

Native or not, the bears have multiplied in the San Bernardinos as the undeveloped land around them has diminished. As a result the word bear crops up time and again in our local papers. The news is always exciting: "Roaming Bears Caught in Yucaipa" one month is followed the next by "Marauding Bears Ransack Oak Glen Candy Store." Then it's "Three Bears Killed After Raids on Oak Glen Petting Zoo" and "Rangers' Darts End Bear of a Visit to Beaumont School." I read "Bear Cub Startles Woman in Tub"; and "Black Bear Visits Banning, Eats Lunch, Heads for Home"; and "Barkley the Bear's Excellent Palm Springs Adventure"; and "Rangers Issue Warnings to Idyllwild Visitors." The conclusion is obvious. Having made their way south, that is, having crossed the Interstate, the tour buses and eighteen-wheelers pounding on either side, black bears have arrived in the San Jacintos. As I write that sentence, I sense waves of ghostly excitement among my cattle-minded predecessors.

Unlike grizzlies, mountain lions have survived the shooting, trapping, poisoning campaigns in a way that is near miraculous. I would like to believe that their place in our mountains is finally secure. Perhaps their secretive habits will make it so. I, for one, have never gotten closer to a lion than the accounts in the *Desert Sun*. Even then, the statistics are unexpected: In 1996 a lion was spotted in an orchard, another one on a golf course. That same year, two lions were killed by motorists, and a third was killed by police. A week later, a lion was found dead in a swimming pool. A few months after that, a lion was found dead on a residential lawn. Some months after that, the residents of a gated community reported mountain lion tracks. "We're in civilization here," Dick Ravet pointed out to the press. "We aren't in the forest. To me, it doesn't make any sense . . . to wait until something happens." Residents were warned to keep a close eye on their poodles.

I always expect to see mountain lions in these mountains, or sure evidence of their presence. They're wonderful creatures, you know, in their place. And this is their place. I only hope they are eating deer and not the lambs of our bighorn sheep. There are plenty of deer, plenty of rodents, lizards, and birds, especially birds. Over the years I have casually checked off scores of sightings: green-tailed towhees, western flycatchers, acorn woodpeckers straight out of Looney Tunes. Stellar's jays; they think they own the place, raging and ruffling up their crests, standing their feathers on end. They are the rowdiest of Peterson's *Western Birds*, all that hollering, the first thing I hear in the morning, the last thing at night. Brown creepers, red-breasted nuthatches, mountain chickadees, little parties of them flirting in the canopy. One time I even spotted a hepatic tanager. At least I think it was a hepatic tanager. I really didn't get a long enough look because my turning the pages from the colored plate of tanagers to the description of tanagers to the range map of tanagers frightened the actual tanager away.

The campground at Round Valley, when I get there, is empty. The previous occupants have thoughtfully left me a tent stake, otherwise my chosen site is bare dirt, with no living plants to be crushed beneath my tent. Although I'm a little embarrassed to be making camp so early, with hours of daylight still left, I thump down my awkward pounds and set up house in cool simplicity. A level spot makes a nice living room: a flat-topped boulder for a table, a log for a chair, half a dozen gooseberry bushes for the walls, a luxuriance of evergreens for the roof. Up goes the tent, the door pitched east for the morning sun. The sleeping bag is fluffed into life, the bundle of extra clothes beaten into the shape of a pillow. My primeval bedroom, a tiny splash of red under the pines.

To feel so tired and yet so fresh! I slip a notebook into my pocket, pour a ration of sunflower seeds into my palm, and go out to admire the scenery from the porch—*porch*, in this instance, meaning a patch of ground under a grandfather pine, between a boulder and a bluebird at his bath. Evergreens absolutely dominate the view: firs, incense cedars, and pines of several kinds, a century of growth in their massive trunks.

Here then is the showcase of a magnificent forest, of which so little remains.

I have learned to look at forests with a critical eye. Only old-growth is good enough, and there must be open aisles where sunlight slants down in broad bars, and a floor littered with needles, cones, and rotting limbs—all that messy fertility exposed. This is what makes the San Jacinto wilderness memorable. And a little fantastic, for in addition to mushrooms, the piney duff has growing out of it some very odd ideas in flowers: the coralroot, for example, in crimson-purple bloom; the fleshy snow plant glowing like a bright red candle; the pinedrop, its whitish blossoms hanging down like bells.

A botanist told me how to tell these pines apart. The ponderosas have cones shaped like beehives. Jeffrey cones are similar in shape, but smaller, and the tree bark has a wonderful smell—what is that smell? Vanilla? Butterscotch? Lodgepole cones are smaller still, by half, and round. Sugar pines have long sticky cones with edible seeds. The sugar, explains J. Smeaton Chase, "is found in the form of grains where wounds have occurred on the trunk. It is medicinal, and should not be used over-freely." The cones of the limber are unremarkable, but some of our limber pines are over two thousand years old, which makes them the oldest living things in the San Jacintos. The Coulter's cones are clawed and monstrous, almost a foot long and heavy, up to five pounds or more. "Widow-makers" the old cowboys called them.

The pines are swathed with an understory of bracken, each fern fully unfurled and strung with the silken threads of spider webs. Lupines, bachelor buttons, and corn lilies embellish the ferns. *Corn lilies*. I'd forgotten about them, how the sunlight

191

defines the veins in their huge leaves, profoundly green, impossibly green, emeralds.

It's hard to say where the corn lilies leave off and the meadow begins, all that tall unmowed grass, with here a patch of flowers, and there an outcrop of granite, and a pathway running around the whole to stretch the legs grown stiff. I gaze at this sequestered spot and think that I'm going to pen some long, wonderfully descriptive literature. I scribble a sentence or two, a paragraph, then a movement catches my eye. Where the forest meets the meadow, one . . . two . . . three mule deer appear, velvety antlered fellows, tails wagging, big mule ears up, mobile, alert. A fourth deer steps out of the shadows, a buck blessed with a dazzling white coat. Such a sight makes the mind go blank with pleasure.

Swirls of air carry my scent to the deer, but they are obviously not inclined to put themselves out in country closed to hunting. They have lost their fear of humans, which is not a good thing to lose. Letting down their long-eared vigilance, they browse untroubled, hard black noses rapturously sunk in the gooseberries. Slowly they move through patches of shade, insofar as I am conscious of them moving at all. Then they melt away like clouds. I search the empty spot where they stood, work my eyes into every shadow, but I see nothing. Meanwhile half an hour of writing time has vanished. Never mind. Having gained my second wind, I cap my pen, stow my notebook, and skip off into the wilderness.

Near the brink of the eastern precipice—never mind the exact location, lets just say, somewhere around here—there's a small elusive body of water called, rather realistically, Hidden Lake. If you didn't already know it was here, you wouldn't know it was here. Fed only by rain and snowmelt, Hidden

Lake is water one year, a dab of oozing meadow the next. Here and nowhere else grows the Hidden Lake bluecurl, a lowly flower of which nobody takes even the slightest notice (if you didn't already know it was here, you wouldn't know it was here). That aside, however, the government just naturally protects the plant by erasing the lake from their maps.

On this El Nino year of water aplenty, the sparkling form of Hidden Lake looks as if it has gotten use to the idea that it's more lake than meadow. The water laps prettily at the knees of the pines. Through rushes and reeds, an assortment of buglife goes about its business of back-swimming, whirligigging, water-striding. More remarkable are the tadpoles—vibrant masses that will become so many thousands, no guessing how many, tiny western toads, long-leggedy and brown. Visualize the trailside scene, thick with toads bravely belly-flopping between your boots, desperate to procreate before the puddles disappear.

Hidden Lake is so appealing that you instinctively reach for your fly rod. But watching is about all you can do, and it's purely out of habit that I search the shallows for fish, the depths for telltale rings. I think, by contrast, of the Idaho backcountry. Now those were real mountain lakes, and we had luck in all of them, Stew and I, the thick-bodied cutthroats hitting everything we tried. But when fish come this big, and so willingly, you always have to be thinking *fish*. You always have to be fishing, your fly rod arcing through the hatches. There is no such thing as spending a lazy afternoon sitting beside a clear little lake just because it's fun. You have to catch fish. And then you have to catch bigger fish. All of nature is fish and how to catch them.

A series of final sunbeams fall on the lake as I rise and head back to camp for my dinner of sardines, sausage, and crackers daubed with globs of cheese. It takes just minutes to prepare. I can do it more quickly but there's no reason to. As it is, with no fish to fry, no dishes to wash, no campfire to feed, no cozily familiar yarns over cups of sweet cocoa, darkness doesn't come early enough. I hang my food sack from a noose of nylon cord hooked over a tree limb, bear high plus two. I treat my blisters and brush my teeth, the only bit of me I can keep clean. I fetch and filter creek water for the morning, then tidy up the tent. That done, I amuse myself in the bird section of my journal, making a fuss to record everything. I stroll into the dusk and stroll back, thus killing ten more minutes. With nothing else to do, nowhere else to go, I tuck myself into the tent to wrestle with insomnia, the sausage gently bubbling in my stomach.

* * *

Dawn finds me shivering, my woolly hat pulled down hard over my ears, my knees hunched up within a foot of my chin, my sleeping bag hauled high over my head, with just a little hole for me to breathe. In hundred-degree weather, it's impossible to see that you'll ever want a down jacket. I'd done well to bring a sweater.

Birdsong ruffles the silence: the *pi-tic, pi-tic, pi-tic* call of a western tanager (probably); the soft mewing of a green-tailed towhee (most likely); the rapid twittering of violet-green swallows (maybe); and the rough, rasping *shook-shook-shook* of Steller's jays (certainly). From the meadow comes the voice of a coyote, calling up the sun like a rooster. It's a hysterical sound, chopped and frantic, "a prolonged howl," to quote an old cowboy, "that the animal lets out, runs after, and bites into small pieces."Thinking to make some subtle sign of friendship, I rise up and give answer. I would have done better to keep silent, for immediately the coyote flees. Not for the first time I have spoiled a relationship with my singing.

The day is full of possibilities, a mountain of possibilities. I'm eager for altitude, and San Jacinto Peak, at 10,804 feet (and growing), will give me a rock solid goal. Fortified by a nutrition bar, I step onto the trail and head for the best view in the world. The breeze, brisk and cool, seems easterly, you can't tell exactly in the mountains; the air wafts up and down, around and back upon itself, while the sky remains un-changed. A few clouds float feathery. The gods are good. No rain. No mosquitoes. No scout troops.

Onward and upward and the ridge reveals a sudden vista, a long sweep of green-hilled distance. Here the trail ends in a T-crossing and two choices are open (this wilderness is so well signed, even I can't go astray). Go north and steeply up for San Jacinto Peak. Go south and steeply down for Saddle Junction—Angels Glide this trail is called, for good reason. A mile down lies Wellman Cienega, an entire mountainside dripping with miniature waterfalls. But its the flowers you tend to remember most, so many and varied are they. *California Mountain Wildflowers* has arranged them all neatly by color: Flowers Reddish, Flowers Whitish, Flowers Bluish, Flowers Yellowish. Reading the field guide makes the flowers all sound dullish. Reading the ground is another matter. From a back-drop of moss rise the yellow heads of monkeyflowers and the lavender lobes of shooting stars. From the ferns rise Indian paintbrush, handsome yellow daisies, and showy blue lupines that are so healthy they grow bush-like, three or four feet high. Here grow the azaleas, especially the azaleas, so heavenly fragrant they make you a little drunk, sensorially. That's six species, a good beginning. You can hunt out and identify the rest yourself.

At Saddle Junction, Angels Glide surrenders itself to Devils Slide, which in turn will deposit you into the mountain communities of Fern Valley and Idyllwild—a clutter of children's camps, tourist lodges, and dozy summer cabins all jammed up against each other, their addresses nailed to the pines. Here the loggers of the past have done their worst work, cut down entire mountainsides for citrus crates and railroad ties. There were no rules in those days, no mitigation measures, no best management practices, no environmental groups arguing over how many timber roads should be cut, how close the roads should be to the creeks, how many trees should be taken, how many left. "It was just cut, cut, cut," as one witness characterized it. "Everybody who could get his hands on a chain saw was butchering the forest." After the better part of a century, the land has somewhat recovered, incredibly, which is better than nothing I suppose.

I knew little of this history in my short time in Idyllwild, a year that was—how to put it?—transforming. Having found a safe if lowly niche in the Los Angeles banking industry, having survived the unbreathable air, the undrinkable water, the traffic, the crime, the Chatsworth/Malibu wildfire, the San Fernando Earthquake, the flood of '69 (at one point I even had Charles Manson for a neighbor), I was ripe for life in a misty alpine village. Living in Los Angeles had given me a lasting desire for solitude. Pine trees, blue skies, gray squirrels . . . That's for me.

Things happen fast in Idyllwild, a lot faster than they happen in Los Angeles. I had made the climb to the village by noon, and by evening I had created the beginning of a completely new life for myself and my two kids. We were residents of Idyllwild, with a year's lease on a lofty A-frame cabin (Bide-a-While) perched on stilts above Strawberry Creek. We had a fridge packed with essentials. We had a post office box, a telephone number, an elementary school, and a subscription to the *Idyllwild Town Crier*. Within days we had the sundeck surrounded with bird feeders, wind chimes, potted strawberry plants, and stacks of split firewood. By the end of the week, it looked as if we had been living in Idyllwild all our lives.

This was happiness, bracketed between forest and creek, of a wild and free sort. So pleased was I with my solitude and my books, I intended to live in that cabin forever, to hide in the coolness of pines. Except that this had been neither a long-considered nor a well-considered move to the mountains. About to sink under a load of overdue bills, I took a red pen to the classified ads in the *Town Crier*. The few jobs that were listed were there for those who wanted them, but I could not see myself making beds and bussing dirty dishes for minimum wage and maximum shifts just for the privilege of living in Idyllwild. It would be drudgery from the first minute to the last. And who knew when that last would come. This wasn't the way it was supposed to end. But perhaps every great adventure needs a false start, a dry run.

From Idyllwild, an hour and dozens of hairpin bends put us back in Palm Springs. For the next eight years, I did more time in a bank, spending long and meaningless hours in uncomfortable high heels, dealing with one paper event after another, my telephone ringing, my ashtray overflowing with Salems from which I'd taken a couple of bored puffs before stubbing them out. A small army of tellers and clerks had been placed under my command, although I never thought of myself as anybody's boss since at times I was hardly my own. This may have made at least marginally easier my decision to quit work for good, this job that after seventeen years I finally recognized as strictly not my line. Then too, I had just met Stew, an Oregon-bred man who likewise had not always done what he was supposed to do. It was one of the odd accidents of my life that I should meet a man in Palm Springs, right out of the blue, whose love of wilderness was as profound as my own.

Suddenly the time was ripe for action, for direct, irresponsible action. There was perhaps a problem about what to say to my boss. "Let's see if I understand you correctly. You are giving up home, career, reputation, medical insurance, and retirement benefits so you can spend the rest of your life plucking berries off a mountainside and talking to wolves?" Well, not entirely. I was also fleeing the permanence of a granite-fronted bank, as well as the narrow boundaries of the desert on which I had been raised but never believed I belonged.

Without much in the way of a backward glance, in full summer heat we set off, Stew driving, for the cool green wilderness of Alaska. *Alaska*—most thrilling of words—where we would lose ourselves, or find ourselves, we didn't know which. There are just some things we have to do before we realize how smart or how dumb they are.

What followed seems like a dream. During the next sixteen years, I found myself living on a patch of mountainside near Challis, Idaho. Stew and I had built the cabin ourselves, log by log, on land we had bought from a couple who were desperate to move to Southern California. Life was simple. Life was good. We followed the seasons and ate generously off the land. We hunted food in the forest, picked food off the bushes, collected food in the leaf litter of the aspen groves, and harvested food in the garden we shared with the deer. Along with this, of course, we had all the fun in the world keeping alive such endangered homesteading skills as tanning buckskin, brewing beer, weaving willow baskets, making berry jam . . . I pounded out the details on a vintage manual typewriter, a daring tale that found its place in Idaho history thanks to Caxton Press (my mother still buys the book and gives it around). How distant that world now seems from a trail in the San Jacintos.

*   *   *

Sensing a peak, my trail climbs steadily, switching back and forth in the general direction of heaven. The tall trees shrink to half size the higher I go. Another mile and the trees stop coming entirely, except in windswept, twisted Krummholz form. While this sounds ruggedly remote, in fact I meet other hikers on their way down, frisky couples wielding wildflower guides and cell phones, most of whom tell me, without being asked, where I am in relation to my destination. Upward, ever upward, I struggle over the boulders. Then suddenly I merge in blessed oblivion with the Great Spirit of Mount San Jacinto. God-like I look out over what an excited John Muir (allegedly) described as "the most sublime spectacle to be found anywhere on this earth!" Actually it's a hundred different views. Beware you who fly in your dreams.

Never have so many contour lines been packed together so closely as on the San Jacinto Peak quadrangle map. My eyes swing across the western panorama, across green hills that rise from the San Jacinto Valley to an arrangement of ridgelines and summits I have never had the energy or ambition to explore. Touched by vertigo, my feet teetering upon their hold at the peak, I swing my eyes across the eastern panorama, across a chaos of canyons running by the dozens to the bone-white, bone-dry bed of the Whitewater River. Even the swallows seem to catch their breath at the drop.

We of the desert must take our rivers as we find them, hard as it is to find them at times. In spring, the melting snowfields of the San Bernardinos flow into the Whitewater; then they sink into the sand before running even a mile. This causes a lot of golf courses to come into being because you can't put houses in a dry riverbed, but you can put in fairways. If they wash away, you simply throw out seeds, wait a week, and tee off as if you knew what you were doing. In truth, the White-water is little more than golf courses strung end to end over the sand, with a stream running several feet underneath.

West of the Whitewater, the San Gorgonio Pass separates the Transverse Range from the Peninsula Range. Not surprisingly, the pass is a funnel for the wind, a mean northern that blows down eucalyptus trees and picks up quantities of sand, keeping Desert Hot Springs continuously on the move. "Open your mouth and she'll blow you wrong side out" is a saying from which residents derive no comfort.

This wind, nothing can stand up to it except the wind machines, and even they have computers that shut them off when gusts spin them rather too wildly. Driving into Palm Springs on Highway 111, you can't help but notice these towers, planted like crops, one row above the other. *Farms* my tour guide called them, because they *grow* electricity. During the first few minutes, he told me more than I ever wanted to know about wind machines, with so much of his effort going into justifying their ugly existence.

Through the pass comes Highway 111. Through the

Coachella Valley it squeezes and fights its way in a continuous bottleneck of traffic. If I let half a year go by without driving from Palm Springs to Indio, on my next trip I feel as though I'm driving an unfamiliar route. So much Colorado desert has been consumed by so much new development, the green ribbons fluttering across the landscape, virtually everything imported, the grass, the flowers, the trees, the low-paid, dark-skinned crews who keep it all from overflowing onto the highway. The names vary—Painted Cove, Park Mirage, Sunterrace (Phase I), Bighorn This and Bighorn That—but the incentives are worded monotonously alike, their references to heated swimming pools, three-car garages, dramatic views, and security gates. It's hard to believe that fifty years ago this wilderness of sand was considered useless, at least for anything developers could think of. But perhaps I'm being too harsh in my judgement. Certainly, all this runs counter to the mood I have brought up the trail.

Late afternoon. Little groups of mountaineers come and go, flushed and hot from their climb. Chattering like starlings, they peel oranges and salt hard-boiled eggs. They grin and strike poses with their walking sticks. Pointing their cameras down, they identify another Coachella Valley entirely, a tamed and orderly nature in a vast empty space waiting to be filled. "Have a good one," they call to me as they leave, and in an unexpected burst of concern someone adds, "Don't get caught in the dark." Half an hour, an hour passes in blissful solitude; apparently I am rooted to my rock. As the sun begins to dip below the lip of the horizon, I heft my rucksack and rise to the warning. By owl-light, I'm picking my way over the rocks, step by dangerously uncertain step . . . evidently in the right direction because I all but stumble onto my tent. Exhausted with the relief of having *made it*, I settle down to a cold dinner that is undeniably perfect.

Languidly I move through the rest of the week, the absurdly sunny days that pass in an expanse of glorious sunrises and sunsets, gruesome nutrition bars and equally gruesome segments of sausage. But rustic bliss has its limits, and I'm as ready as anyone to return to the land of lighted rooms, wholesome meals, soft beds, and bubble baths. Paradise or no paradise, I know the meaning of Sunshine Villas at last. God, that I should sell out so.

I look at the disorganized mountain of gear on the forest floor and I heave a huge sigh. I dump half of it into the main sack of the Kelty, stick my foot in, stomp a few times, and dump in the rest. Down the trail I bolt; when my goal is near, I pick up my pace. By noon I'm climbing the concrete ramp by which way I have come seemingly months ago.

SIX

At Large in Skunk Cabbage Meadow

Slug-abeds were shaken from their ease Thursday morning at 8:55 by the strongest earthquake recorded in Palm Springs for the past ten years [6.0 centered in Anza]. No damage was reported although local streets were peopled by nervous ladies in French nightgowns who leaped from their beds without one longing, lingering look behind.

—THE LIMELIGHT NEWS 1937

A PERSON WHO IS tired of August is not necessarily tired of life; it might be the heat. As a matter of course, the thermometer sticks above 110 degrees in the shade and rarely drops below 80 in the night. The humidity, of course, makes it feel even hotter, and nowhere is there any feeling of a breeze.

In an effort to keep the heat hidden under a wide-brimmed hat, the city of Palm Springs urges its weather forecasters to avoid using such offensive terms as *sizzling, scorcher,* and the detested *yowza.* And yet tax records show that today's tourists apparently do like it hot. The Desert Shadows Inn, for example, has been fully booked every weekend this summer, all thirty of its guests bobbing merrily in the pool in the yowza noontime sun. Gone are the negative images of my childhood summers, the dead lawns, the swimming pools inert, the parking meters capped with paper sacks, the tinfoil crimped in the shop windows to ward off the sun, the signs saying See You In October.

But not for me, this sun. After breakfast and the news, I retreat to my bedroom, pull down the shades, turn on the lights, and pretend it's raining. I try to stay hard at work because there is absolutely nothing else to do but work. Work, and never think about the mountain, how a week up there can bring about a miracle of rejuvenation.

I think about the mountain. Possible camping sites fix themselves in my mind: Skunk Cabbage Meadow, Tahquitz Valley, Lower Basin, North Rim, Desert View, Chinquapin—all of which have the happy distinction of lying within the wilder-seeming San Jacinto Wilderness, where I can pitch my tent almost anywhere, have a campfire if I like, bring a dog if I have one . . . not that I'm likely to get one, mind you, lest my mother tire of me as a roommate, indigent that I am. An odious and graceless thought. An August thought. High time to be off.

So: Make a list. Go to the grocery store, the sporting goods store, the map store. Make another list. Another trip to the grocery store. Pack. Repack. Gulp a hasty breakfast. Slam out the door. Turn around. Grab a hat. Turn back on Mother and Home.

* * *

August in the San Jacintos is glorious, warm in the sun, cool in the shade. Stoking myself with sunflower seeds, I hike to my destiny at a steady mile per hour, load humped against my back, bare legs pasted with sun block, DEET, and mashed flies. The trail goes steeply up, which is bad, then steeply down, which is worse. Up. Down. Up. And then, by golly, down again. Skunk Cabbage Meadow beckons and the boots keep moving, putting a steadily increasing distance between me and civilization.

Someone named it Skunk Cabbage Meadow without looking skunk cabbage up. These are corn lilies, and they are virtually odorless and look nothing like cabbages. What is even worse, the misidentified corn lily continues to be misidentified as skunk cabbage because of the meadow's name, a mistake that has caused unfortunate consequences over the years. As a young shoot, the skunk cabbage, which is edible, looks like the corn lily, which is poisonous, or it looks enough like it to occasionally require the evacuation of a boy scout.

To the northeast of Skunk Cabbage Meadow lies a forested bench called Laws Camp in commemoration of George Law, a freelance journalist who built a cabin on the site in 1916. Law meant his cabin to be a part of the mountain, simple, primitive, just the bare-handed basics. The walls were stone slabs laid as flat as they had lain in the earth, thick or thin as the spot demanded, in varying shades just as they came to hand from the stacks. The ridgepole and rafters were hewed from nearby cedars and pines, so the roof fitted the walls in an irregular way. Meadow grass covered the roof, wild-sown with buttercups, so it turned yellow in June, further binding the cabin to the earth. To his everlasting credit, Law used no ready-mix, no window glass, no chinking other than grass. He didn't turn the meadow into a pasture for livestock. He didn't divert the creeks, so they continued to flow where they wished, and deer drank from them instead of cows.

Working alone, how long did it take Law to build the cabin? Three seasons? Six? Stonework isn't something that lends itself to hurry and speed. No doubt he muttered to himself the usual entreaties: There's no need to go at this great guns, working yourself to a bloody pulp. It isn't going to get finished in one summer, so you might as well come to understand the process. Like using the heavier stones first, down low, lifting them no higher than necessary. And using the flat stones on top and the square stones on corners. So okay, it was possible, stone cabins could be built. He could do it.

Although a mason's eye must follow a wall precisely, his thoughts are free to veer off in any direction. So with his pipe drawing nicely, Law was able to delve into life, letting subjects come and go at will. With some people, the busier their hands are somewhere else the better they work in their head—which fortunately was the part that earned Law a living. I imagine an entry in his journal might read, "I have had a productive day: twenty stones and two thousand words."

Cabin-building and wool-gathering. But that wasn't all that went on around there. Living steadily outdoors, Law was able to gain an intimacy with the place, to learn the habits and schedules of the deer who came daily to the creek, were admired, and perhaps named, and the jays who filched his bacon, and the chipmunks who whisked off his crumbs, and the squirrels who watched the strong shell of his cabin grow stone by stone.

Even with frequent breaks to relight, refill, or simply find his pipe, Law managed to finish the walls, the floor, and the roof before he ran out of energy. Besides that, the cabin looked like it was supposed to look, that is, as if it had been thrown out of the ground. The only hitch was that it stood on land that Law had leased from the Southern Pacific Railroad for ten dollars a year. So he never really owned the cabin, except in his head and by his sweat, and by that time the cabin owned him too, his affection.

Law lived in the San Jacintos for ten seasons—plenty of time for a literary democrat to become a narrow-minded property owner at odds with everyone who plucked *his* gooseberries, caught *his* fish, shot *his* deer. At some point, he must have caught an extreme case of wanderlust, for he left the San Jacintos and never returned, thus cutting short my favorite story. For years thereafter, his byline was found attached to Mexican travel yarns in the Automobile Club's *Westways*.

The wild creatures seemed not to miss him any more than they had minded him. As soon as he turned his back, the mice moved in and plundered the bedding for feathers. Time worked its mischief on the roof, and the swallows flew in with bugs in their beaks. The chinking lost its grip, and the stone walls, weakened by wayward roots, collapsed with neglect. So by the time the Forest Service got around to knocking the cabin down it didn't have all that far to fall. Thus what had been the focus of one man's life vanished off the face of the earth, giving no truth that anyone had ever lived there.

And yet . . . I wanted to find the truth of that cabin. Even in ruins it had to be here, a dooryard path, perhaps, or the posts of a porch or the crumbled remains of a chimney, where the smoke of many a pipe dream once rose. But there wasn't a ruin in sight. Maybe I was searching too far east. Maybe the creeks had changed course. Maybe too many years had stacked up between me and the press clipping I held in my hand. Then suddenly, on a bench above the confluence of Willow Creek and Tahquitz Creek, I had a cornerstone at my feet, a granite boulder that looked exactly like the one I had pictured in my hand. And there, almost hidden in bushes and ferns, where heaps of smooth flat stones lay in disorderly lines, lay George Law's cabin.

When on that day last August I pitched camp beside the cabin site, it was like any August day a hundred years ago. The smell of the pines was the same. The spring where I knelt and plunged my head was George Law's sweet little spring, and I came away from it all fresh and glowing with the cold as he had. The sun I watched set, round and red, and the moon I watched rise, yellow and bright in the green twilight, were his as well. I settled there for three days and pretended nothing had changed.

* * *

East of Laws, where the forest drops abruptly, shockingly to the desert floor, there lies a mountain camp where you can watch the stars come on above you and the lights come on below. Caramba the mapmakers called it, Spanish for "great guns!" referring to the view. In 1916 Moses Gordon camped here while he was building a trail that would link his cabin in the desert with his cabin in the mountains. Sometimes he spent whole weeks at Caramba, tucked away in this place that some would called desolate.

The trail cost Gordon "a full thousand dollars cash" to build and two years of his life, most of which was spent pickaxing basically straight up the granite escarpment. Drudgery indeed. All to no avail. Because even though the press appreciated the trail, turning it into "a shortcut from the desert to the snow, the palms to the pines, the Equator to the North Pole," the public did not. The Great Hiking Era had come to an end. In fact, so little was the trail used, the chaparral soon closed in and made it all but impassable. As for Gordon, someone must know what happen to him, but I don't. My research simply petered out.

Southwest of Caramba, you'll find two flower-strewn bowls that go by the name of Tahquitz Valley and Little Tahquitz Valley. In a fit of enthusiasm, the mapmakers have taken hold of the name Tahquitz and applied it to a peak, a creek, a canyon, a waterfall, and a wash. Even that isn't the end of it. You can tee off at Tahquitz Creek Golf Resort, get tested for cataracts at Tahquitz Optical, and have your poodle shampooed at Tahquitz K-9 Country Club. Tahquitz. *Takwish*. Taaa-quits you say if you grew up in Palm Springs, accent on the first wild syllable.

Tahquitz is the perfect Cahuilla villain in that he assumes so many forms, there's no guessing how many. He's lightning, he's flood, he's the wild north wind. He's a condor, an ogre, a giant, neither jolly nor green. He's a hermit standing beside the trail, a dark obtrusive presence, subtly, defiantly not human. As you glance over your shoulder you no doubt wonder where he came from, where he lives. Where else but in Tahquitz Canyon, way up there in the cavernous reaches. It makes you wonder why people say, "Oh, Tahquitz Canyon is so beautiful," why it has any reputation beyond fearsome. It's also odd that the word true believers use to describe their feelings for Tahquitz is respect. You have to respect Tahquitz. In my mind, a spirit worthy of respect does not launch forth into the night as a meteoric star, catch up your sleeping infant, carry it to a mortar hole, and mill it to pulp.

Central to the myth of Tahquitz, and several degrees of magnitude more troubling, is what appears to be his power to shake up the earth. Such imagery is hardly surprising, given the huge power of plate tectonics, the shifting of plates along the San Andreas Fault. So active is this fault, all who live a full span in our desert have earthquake stories to tell, some of which take on wondrous proportions through the years. More reliable is the picture Francisco Patencio presents:

> One time (I was very small, I could not remember yet), there came such earthquakes as had not been known to any of the people. Whole mountains split—some rose up where there had been none before. Other peaks went down and never came up again. It was a terrible time. The mountains that the people knew well were strange places that they had never seen before.

This, say Cahuilla historians, was the 1857 Fort Tejon earthquake, the strongest earthquake (at an estimated magnitude 8.3) to hit Southern California in recorded history. From Marysville to San Diego to Las Vegas, talk throughout the shell-shocked countryside focused on the quake, and anyone willing to be interviewed, was interviewed, again and again:

> The earth was in fearful agitation, with undulations so quick and rapid as to make it almost impossible to stand.

> The solid earth seemed to have lost its stability and a wave-like motion was experienced as on shipboard . . . For a moment nature seemed filled with terror.

> The ground gaped in places a width of eight or ten feet, closing again immediately, like the snap of some earth demon's jaw. A prospector, who had passed the night under the Tejon oaks, was frightened to his feet by the shock just in time to see his blankets and rifle swallowed up and buried forever as the rent closed upon them.

I read of rivers flowing backward, of rivers thrown out of their beds, of the ground fracturing for hundreds of miles "across valleys, through lakes, and over hills, without regard to inequality or condition of surface." And as I read, it came to me that if such a blow were to strike the Coachella Valley today . . . well, we just might find out. As recently as last Tuesday, the ground shook, not much, but enough to rattle windows and set us here at Sunshine Villas to murmuring. It was over in seconds, damaged nothing, killed no one, and disappeared from memory shortly thereafter. But let me quickly add that I am always ready for the day when that casual shaking suddenly becomes the great earthquake of the decade. If you can believe scientists, the Coachella Valley is indeed a scary place to live. In fact, our sixty-mile segment of the San Andreas Fault has such potential for seismic violence, one local newspaper includes a weekly earthquake supplement with columns devoted to survival techniques for the home, to intelligence about canned food, bottled water, and tents, to instructions for shutting off the gas, cooking on a camp stove, and sanitizing human waste.

So how big will the Big One be? My sources do not entirely agree, but taken together they cast light on the overall picture. With shifting amounts of dread and concern, I see freeway overpasses crashing down, stranding thousands of spectators at the Nabisco Championship. I see structural failure at the Palm Desert mall, my brother Jim, proud owner of Record Alley, buried beneath his New Selections. I see phone lines going dead, lights going dark, gas mains breaking, fires erupting . . . Mom and I in our nightgowns, broad-jumping fissures, running for our lives.

Even so, every day thousands of motorists cross our segment

of the fault unaware. No monument marks the spot. No road map draws its course. You can't really say that here is the North American Plate and right over there is the Pacific Plate; the actual plate boundaries are not so sharply defined. But look down from the snug cabin of an airplane and you'll see the fault lined out in spooky strips of riparian greenery: Two Bunch Palms, Seven Palms, Thousand Palms, Willis Palms, Hidden Palms, Pushawalla Palms, Biskra Palms . . . Set in an expanse of glaring white sand, these oases are uncommonly pretty. People go there to live, never in their wildest dreams imagining they have bought directly over a fault. And real estate agents are understandably silent.

What is unmistakable, however, is the fault's penchant for pushing mountains around. The San Jacinto Range, a monstrous example of plate tectonics, is still rising, still active, still at play with the Richter scale. Seven miles in, and the trail through Skunk Cabbage Meadow continues firmly as if my stopping doesn't matter. "Camp," I say, feeling like the oldest backpacker in the world.

* * *

Dawn, and the meadow goes bright. Breakfast over, I circle my map with a medley of destinations. I step onto the trail and across a creek that the mapmakers have classified intermittent and left unnamed. Only in wet times does it run, slipping dreamily through scoops of green meadow, as if, like me, there is nowhere it has to be. Willow Creek, on the other hand, is classified perennial even though it's hardly deep enough to float a fish. After starting life as a series of springs at Wellman Cienega, it twists and turns through the willows, picking up Tahquitz Creek and odd trickles of water that come angling in from the north. Upon reaching the escarpment, over the edge and down the canyon they all go, crashing, falling, losing themselves in sandy oblivion at the base.

Tahquitz Creek is remarkable for its lemon lilies, tremendously scented, the nostrils positively quiver. Lemon lilies look for all the world like they dropped from heaven, and no camera can do them justice. Nevertheless, I take my wildflower lens from its black leather pouch and twist-click it into place. Bending, stooping, lens-twiddling, I look into the viewfinder and squeeze the shutter repeatedly. I know I'm trying for a shot that's impossible, but lemon lilies are why I lug around fifteen pounds of camera gear.

My trail soon parts company with the creeks and settles down to a smooth, level stride. Officially I'm on the Pacific Crest Trail—the PCT we fondly call it—a corridor that wends its way from the Canadian border to the Mexican border. All in all, from end to end, it would take a free spirit about five months of savage walking to complete the trail (and $900 in topo maps), the thought of which takes the glory out of my own trip at a stroke.

A turn or two takes me far out on the rim of the escarpment. Here the trail clings to the very ledge and is in some danger of dropping off altogether. The uphill side is strewn with boulders, some of which have obviously fallen not long ago. The few conifers still standing have been reduced to naked spars, easily pushed over by hand one thinks. The downhill side, by contrast, is thick with great folds of chaparral, the *brush* in brush fires. "Elfin forest" the early promoters tagged it when they were hunting for romantic terms. Some forest! In moments you find yourself wedged among masses of leathery leaves, fuzzy flowers, dusty berries, and tortuous, interlocking branches, your clothes torn, your flesh bleeding, your sense of direction quite gone. Actually you don't even consider going in; you just look down at it. And down is where it's all going very quickly. It occurs to me that walking here at exactly the wrong seismic moment is tantamount to sudden and sure annihilation.

Southeast from where I stand, twenty miles away in distance and a hundred years away in time, lies Vandeventer Flat. *Se-o-ya* the Cahuillas called it, pleasant view. In the early 1920s, as he was preparing his joyously energetic travel book *The Southern Sierras of California*, Charles Francis Saunders, accompanied by a neighbor he calls the Professor, stumbled into this mile-high scoop of valley while they were tracing the route of the Anza Party. (Captain Juan Bautista de Anza, you might remember, led the first civilian expedition from Sonora, Mexico, to San Francisco, a legendary trek across uncharted deserts and mountains.) After urging their complaining burros up Coyote Canyon, "a widish, sunny, inviting way," Saunders and the Professor forced them up Horse Canyon, where "troubles began to accumulate." Horse Canyon in life was horribly different than Horse Canyon on paper. Now jabbed by cactus, now stumbling over broken rocks, they pressed on, the legs of their burros feeling nervously for footholds. With a desperate effort on everybody's part, they finally arrived at Vandeventer Flat, where the wind was blowing "shrewd and nippingly." Drawing up to an old deserted cabin wherein they would spend the night, Saunders observed: "Hither a half-century ago came one Vandeventer out of the desert."

I spent months trying to piece together the several bits of Frank Vandeventer's story. As an adventurous bachelor, he had made a series of moves through New York, San Francisco, and the San Gorgonio Pass before entering Palm Springs history in the 1870s as keeper of the stage station, where, as Saunders suggests, he "dispensed refreshment . . . largely liquid and alcoholic . . . to travelers suffering discomfort from the desert's dust and heat." Typically these travelers were footloose young men with broad shoulders and few qualms about hard, disagreeable labor. They were gold miners, most of them, lured to the Colorado River by distorted reports they wanted so much to believe. As usual, they met a rough reality. After going through all the work and expense of getting to the mines, they then had to borrow money for stage fare back home.

Due to the double necessity of keeping within reach of water and out of reach of Indians, the distance the stages actually traveled exceeded that specified in the contracts. George Wharton James was amazed that these contracts continued "in spite of the bad habit contracted by the Indians of personally undertaking to distribute not only the mails, but the dead bodies of the mail carriers, the mail coaches, and the stock . . . and the occasional playful acts of impaling the station keepers with arrows and spears."

In turn, five contractors (or seven, depending on your source) ran from San Bernardino to the Colorado River—three days there, three days back. Nothing moved easily over that distance, a harsh and changeless landscape varied only by eroded gullies and long stretches of soft sand that could and did engulf coaches. These were the rough miles of the Bradshaw Route, a road that was not yet a road but the frailest wagon track marked by the bones of played-out pack animals and crisscrossed with Indian trade routes that pointed in every direction, confusing things. Directly ahead was nothing. Farther ahead was the Colorado River, the end of the road. It too was nowhere, but it was where the coaches were headed, somehow, sometime.

As mining activity shifted, so did the quality of the stages. That is, as traffic increased they progressed from weekly "mud wagons" pulled by mules to daily "coaches and six." They were imposing cradles on wheels, these Concord coaches (so called from Concord, New Hampshire), able to accommodate over a dozen passengers, with an undetermined number on the roof and nine seated inside, or not so much seated as jammed hip to hip, knee to knee, making for a grueling journey, even if by rare good fortune no one smoked, or smelled cheesily in need of a bath, or belched the fumes of Vandeventer's refreshments. Yet if you think of these coaches at all these days, you think of the plush silk upholstery, the bright red paint, the gilt scrolls and fruit clusters on the doors, all of which gave passengers the impression they were about to set out on a festive journey. But that's not the way it worked. As the coaches moved into less-settled country, the stage stations took on the character of the route, and the driver hooted his horn upon arrival only for his own amusement.

Nothing is more discouraging than being in a bad place and being told that another place—your next stop—is a great deal worse. As witnessed by several note-taking survivors, these desert stations were no more than waterholes, and the water-holes were no more than holes in the ground, as the jingle of their names suggests: Chuckwalla Well, nicknamed Choke-for-Water Well. Indian Wells, "a square, boarded-up well, with rope and buckets all complete." Martinez, where water was procured "by a very tedious process." Canyon Spring, closed to one party "by a dead horse, whose fly-covered carcass block-ades the narrow entrance and forbids our reaching water." In reality, no name would do for these stations. What were they? Nothing.

Set down in a desert that was without law, without even the pretense of law, Vandeventer's stage station gave notice that the journey would get worse before it got better. If the passengers were looking for a meal, a bath, a barber, a bed, they were sorely disappointed. The station itself was "wattle and daub," that is, built of bushes and branches laced tightly together and slapped over with a thick primordial mud collected conveniently close to the building site. The floor was beaten earth packed hard under the heel. The window was a square hole without glass, a commodity difficult to transport safely by buckboard and easily destroyed when put to use. The furniture, I imagine, was as simple as furniture could be and still merit the name: a cot, a bare pine table, several three-legged stools, with perhaps a little stove in one corner, a little cupboard in another, and never to be left out, a wash-up basin, a yellow bar of soap, and a dirty towel hung from a peg. Nothing would have made the station interesting because nothing could. Those low-slung adobes did not lend themselves to decoration. But they were practical; the walls, three feet thick, were cool in the summer, warm in the winter, and above all, bulletproof.

Nothing would be harder to describe or more boring to read than Vandeventer's life in Hellhole, California. "A year passed," someone writes, and there is no tedium in the phrase, no intense heat, no intolerable wind, no punishing solitude. "Another year passed"—how hard to imagine the dark and funless nights, the bugle challenging the silence, blasting into your dreams. Then a momentary flash of activity, the frenzied work of exchanging the exhausted team for fresh, of playing host to a coachload of short-tempered strangers. Then a cloud of dust and the stage is gone, and the whole world gone with it. But perhaps I've got it wrong. Perhaps Vandeventer's banishment to this outpost, this life of carefree bachelordom, isn't to be pitied. Perhaps he was at home here among a handful of peaceful Cahuilla Indians as he was never at home in white society. Perhaps he required this spiritual refuge, these expanses of utter quietness that only the sparrows could penetrate. It's hard to know what to think. Vandeventer was a silent man in the history books, if you don't count Saunder's story.

Whatever the case, this solitary life I have been describing took a surprising turn the day two Yaqui Indians walked into Vandeventer's world, an old gentleman and his daughter, a dusky angel "of so great comeliness that Vandeventer took a fancy to her"—we have the word of Saunders on that. She must have behaved as sweetly as she looked, because following the "disgraceful custom" of the time Vandeventer proposed to the father to buy her. "The old Indian, however, who seems to have been the better civilized of the two, refused to do this unless the suitor would marry the girl. 'That's all right,' said Vandeventer, 'here's a padre now; let's settle it.'"

That padre would be Hank Brown, now remembered, if at all, as the "whip" of the Bradshaw Route for almost the entire span of the stage's history. Like all those capable drivers who occur from time to time in worthy novels, Brown was well aware of his responsibilities: the expensive coaches and horseflesh, the shipments of gold, the parties of nervous passengers, none of whom enjoyed the experience except in the retelling of it. Just as certainly, Brown had the audacity to cross any desert, however wild, to climb any mountain, however high, to fight any Indian, however savage. For everyone aboard, disaster was diverted almost hourly through his skill with horses. In fact, he was so good, the passengers decided there was little—nothing—to driving a stage because the horses did it all.

Hank Brown, endowed with all the qualifications of a good stage man, enjoyed the role he played. Smooth-shaven and rotund, he did a good imitation of a padre when a padre was called for. Composing his carnal features into a look of long-suffering piety, he raised his arms, mumbled "some hocus-pocus" over the couple, and pronounced them man and wife. Then ceasing to look either holy or radiant, Brown took himself away; he had a stage to catch.

Frank Vandeventer's story would have ended here had not the railroad arrived. But there's no stopping progress, of course. And although the stage survived marginally for a few more years, continued to run as if the habit were too strong to break, its fate became one with the pony express. When the last stage company went out of business, Vandeventer gathered up his ladylove, to whom he was now thoroughly and legally married, climbed the old Palm Canyon trail, and set up housekeeping on the reservation of the Santa Rosa Band of Cahuilla Indians. Here was a land of milk and honey, by the looks of it, of bear rugs and squirrel hats, of venison stew and quail on toast, in or out of season. So here the Vandeventers built their cabin and devoted the rest of their years to raising two sons "in the usual fashion of the mountain people." Which means they probably raised all kinds of Cain with their wild surroundings.

In a way, our interest is compelled as much by the brothers Vandeventer as by their father. Of the sons, one was dubbed, with typical village scorn, a peculiar man. Charlie *was* strange. History presents two images. The first creates an odd scene at the meeting hall in Anza Valley, the young dark-skinned Charlie hanging by his legs from the crossbeam of the roof, his face squeezed into a fiddle, his bow scratching out "Turkey in the Straw." The second image is of Charlie making happy play with nitroglycerin, knocking the daylights out of his relatives and occasionally blowing away the better part of his own eyebrows. In those older, free-ranging days, mountain people used explosives regularly to rid themselves of poorly placed boulders and tree stumps, as well as marauding grizzly bears (bait a log with honey, wire it with nitroglycerin, and stand clear). Making a big bang, I suppose, may also have passed for fun.

After their father died, the brothers Vandeventer were evicted from the home place, and by the grace of Washington the Santa Rosa Band was allowed back to live out "the placid twilight of its existence." But that isn't to say the Vandeventers' tenure in the mountains was over. As long-time residents, they were perfect for the job of government ranger. The offer was this: a salary of $50 a month, a new cabin, a supply of food, a string of pack horses, and a license to roam their neck of the woods (should they happen to spot a rising plume of smoke, the area ranchers were sure to turn out any time, day or night). No young man could turn down such an offer, especially the homeless Vandeventers.

* * *

Further east and south from where I stand lies a lively mosaic of irrigated fields, date groves, catfish ponds, and at the very edge of the earth, the Salton Sea. It's a heck of a place to put a sea but there it lies, a miracle of water that mocks the surrounding desert by being saltier than the ocean. Actually the Salton Sea isn't a sea, no matter what it looks like. It's a lake, the largest in California, a de facto wetland created in 1905 by human error. Thirty-five miles long, it lies tidelessly in what is called the Salton Trough, an elongated tectonic depression extending (approximately) from Palm Springs to the head of the Gulf of California.

Historically, the shifty waters of the Colorado River have given birth to a succession of Salton Seas, that is, to a succession of temporary fresh-water lakes in the Salton Trough. Sometimes the river would flow south off its silty delta and into the gulf, in which case, the water in the trough would evaporate, leaving a marsh, salty and doomed. Sometimes the river would flow north off its delta and into the trough, creating another fresh-water lake. Collectively these lakes (there were at least six) are called *Ancient* Lake Cahuilla to differentiate them from the small, modern, man-made Lake Cahuilla near La Quinta.

Teams of scientists have been busy along the shoreline of the last Ancient Lake Cahuilla, grabbing the last clues before this world class archaeology site is lost under country clubs and strip malls. Their accounts refer to the strange alignments of stone called fish traps where aboriginal Cahuillas harvested the mullet, suckers, chubs, and trout that migrated into the lake by way of the Colorado River. *Par-powl* the Indians called their lake, waters bewitched.

More obvious than the fish traps are the surrounding hillsides where hundreds of miles of old beach lines remain starkly vivid, as though washed by waves only yesterday. Below the hillsides, shells cover the ground "like dirty snow," varying in size "from a pinhead to a small grain of rice" to "kernels of corn" to "mussel shells two inches long." The words are those of Frances Anthony, and although his observations were written a century ago they fully reflect reality today. Note the name Coachella Valley, Valley of the Conchilla, the little shell. The mapmakers, so one story goes, unfamiliar with the Spanish tongue, misspelled *conchilla* and the valley has been misspelled ever since. "They have given our beautiful valley a bastard name," bleated one pioneer, "without meaning in any language!"

In the decades before 1905, if you had visited the Salton Sink—as the dry lake bed was called—you would have seen a marsh, neither beautiful nor fresh, encrusted with salt a foot thick in places and sufficiently pure to attract caravans of salt-seekers from La Reina de los Angeles, the sleepy adobe village we call Los Angeles today. Much later, a branch line of the Southern Pacific rose from the marsh and with it the New Liverpool Salt Company, a small factory of sorts that provided employment for hundreds of Cahuilla Indians. *Employment?* Yes, but the conditions in which they worked— the mundane, repetitive effort, the glaring salt fields, the sun blazing down without letup—suggested forced labor. What agonies those men suffered, plowing the salt, raking it into cones, drying it, grinding it, sorting it, sacking it, loading it onto boxcars for shipment to the coast. Yet in such conditions was salt manufactured.

So before 1905 the Salton Sink was salt and it was marsh and it was a giant pothole of ooze. It was hot springs, hotter mud pools, and boiling caldrons of quicksand. It was a lunar thrust of volcano cones that assaulted the nose of George Wharton James:

> The smell of sulphur was quite strong, and the bubbling, soughing, hissing, venting, and spitting of the water,

steam, and mud filled our ears. There were over a hundred vents of one kind or another, most of them so small as to be perfectly ridiculous . . . The tiniest of some of the vents was a source of amusement to me, for they were so small that my lead pencil effectively checked their spitting and fizzling. I thrust it down one of them as far as it would go, and when it was withdrawn the little crater, or cone, like a vicious cat, spat and hissed at me.

At the same time, incredibly, somewhere within this lava landscape emerged a developer's dream of an agricultural wonderland where crops could be grown twelve months of the year. All that stood in the way was the lack of significant rainfall (2.4 skimpy inches a year is average). Those clever old real estate rascals. They might just as well have been dreaming of Palm Valley before the Big Drought, except that in this case, tantalizing amounts of water from the Colorado River were running wasted into the gulf.

It made perfect sense. Just turn the river around and send it where it was needed. The vision was as old as it was new, dating back to 1860 when Dr. Oliver M. Wozencraft, San Bernardino's leading citizen (and ardent irrigationist, if only in his imagination), suggested this very thing, pressing his case before Congress for nearly three decades, to no avail. The river itself would suggest the best path, that is, a big braided channel called the Alamo River (historically the Colorado also had a liking for another channel called the New River). The land proposed for development was mostly below sea level, hence gravity would virtually eliminate the cost and complications of dams, booster pumps, and other engineering accessories. Half our trouble, fretted George Chaffee, president of the California Development Company (CDC, to use the vernacular), is the picture people have of a salt-layered sink, a barren ugly desert. Let's forget Salton Sink and give the place a pleasant name. Imperial *Valley*. *Imperial* Valley. *Imperial*, as in empire, for the millions of acres of farmland irrigated water would seize from the desert.

The CDC moved fast and cut many corners, just how many history has not forgotten. After only six months of construction and a mere $100,000 in cost, head gates were raised and the waters of the Colorado River were detoured into a forty-mile ditch that carried life to the Salton Sink. Dredges, plows, and mule-drawn scoops had tamed the river for the very first time. Now the promoters went to work. Having wisely eliminated such ominous words as *desert* and *sink*, they borrowed the old tried and true adjectives of the railroad pamphlets. Then they added a few of their own, even going so far as to compare the Imperial Valley to the Egyptian Delta, the Colorado River to its Nile. Equally exaggerated were the potential yields per acre, the blessings of the soil so fertile from ancient floods. The Homestead Act was also part of the deal. Here was the last chance in California to claim free land, and a daily train brought homesteaders to claim it. Soon there were two daily trains, then three. Not since the gold rush had there been such a boom. Fortunes were made overnight.

Almost everything the homesteaders tried *did* grow. At Imperial, Calexico, Brawley, Holtville, Heber, and El Centro, tent cities sprang up out of nowhere in no time. In turn, the tents were replaced with brave little cottages as fast as the mule teams could bring in lumber. Even as the ranchers of Palm Valley were suffering through the final years of the Big Drought, the farmers of Imperial Valley were celebrating every milestone in growth, the first barber shop, the first post office, the first school, the first bank, the first newspaper.

In 1900, before developed water arrived, the population of Imperial Valley hovered around a dozen, and not an acre was under cultivation. By 1904 more than eight thousand settlers were tramping the dusty streets and seventy-five thousand acres were under cultivation. Developed water had made possible a lot of what was called Progress but later would be called something else. These people had no idea what they were in for. In a word, the trouble was silt. The Colorado has always been one of the siltiest rivers in the world, and now it had a new dumping ground for all that silt. Almost from the start, irrigation managers struggled to keep intakes, canals, and distribution ditches open. And still the silt kept building to dangerous levels, choking the main canal so it could no longer carry the volume of water needed by an ever-increasing number of irrigators. Blame was laid. Charges were filed. The courts saw plenty of action. It was bad publicity, and bad publicity could cut off the stream of immigrants that boosters and valley leaders considered essential to their well being. So, after "mature deliberation," another intake was cut into the west bank of the river, four miles south of the Mexican border, thus allowing the water to bypass the silted-up portions of the main canal. Solutions can generate their own problems, but this one may be something of a record.

In previous decades the Colorado River had produced only three winter floods, and never two in the same year. But wouldn't you know it, in this vital winter of 1905, it produced three separate floods—a by-product of what we would view today as a phase of El Nino. Add to this the unusual floods of that spring and the always-expected floods of summer, and there you have it: the river all set to rearrange the Imperial Valley to its own liking. And that it did. It broke through the new ill-timed Mexican intake. Then obeying the demand of gravity, it headed helter-skelter, by way of its old channels, the New and Alamo Rivers, for the lowest point in the Salton Sink. In "blind, undirected, uncontrollable fury," to quote George Wharton James, the river ran northward unchecked; the *whole* of the Colorado River, "gathered in Utah, Wyoming, Colorado, New Mexico, Nevada, Arizona, and California." It rushed over waterfalls of its own making. It undercut its own banks at every bend. It tore out bridges, inundated telegraph poles, drowned railway stations, and made off with forty miles of Southern Pacific track. It obliterated all traces of the salt-works: the town, the mill, the fields (more lawsuits were filed). It washed away part of Calexico and most of Mexicali (survivors were seen huddled on the few clumps of ground that showed above sheets of water). It took out fences, flushed out farmers, destroyed thousands of acres of farmland, and so eroded thousands more, they could never be cultivated again. Well, that was it for raising lettuce.

Meanwhile a small band of engineers and an army of workmen were doing their best to stop the runaway river. But everything they tried was torn away by a series of new floods that drowned an even broader stretch of perfectly good desert. Although engineers are basically resilient, some of them opted to let the river take over the whole damn valley, the entire empire, think of it!

More reasonable men agreed that an engineering genius was called for. And the Southern Pacific Railroad had that genius, Harry T. Cory (and not so incidentally, a lot of money to throw around). With a frantic effort, Cory fought the flood.

Or to put it graphically, with an army two-thousand strong, recruited partly from California, partly from Mexico, and partly from half a dozen southwest Indian tribes. With ten work trains, a thousand flatcars, and three hundred side-dump cars, Cory fought the flood. With steam shovels, pumps, pile drivers, steel cable, and dynamite. With rock quarried from hundreds of miles around, with clay from Mexico, with gravel from the Southern Pacific's "Mammoth Pit." With a forest of heavy timbers and thousands of cords of brush, Cory fought the flood and lived (barely) to tell about it:

> For three weeks, two divisions of the Southern Pacific, embracing about 200 miles of main line, was practically tied up because of the demand for equipment and facilities . . . and shipping from San Pedro was practically abandoned for two weeks until we returned a considerable portion of the equipment. It was a case of putting rock into the break faster than the river could take it away. In 15 days after we got the trestle across and dumped the first carload of rock we had the river stopped. In that time we handled rock faster than it was ever handled before.

F. H. Dewell, the director of reclamation, gives us a clear picture of the final moments of this, the seventh effort to plug the break:

> The stones used were as large as could be handled or pushed from the flat cars by a gang of men, or by as many men as could get around a stone. The scene at the closure of the break was exciting. Train after train with heavy locomotives came to the place and the stones, large and small, were pushed off by hundreds of workmen as rapidly

as the cars could be placed. Added to the roar of the waters were the whistle signals, the orders to the men, and the bustle of an army working day and night to keep ahead of the rapid cutting of the stream. Then finer material was added and rapidly piled up on the accumulated rock mass. By thus piling up finer and finer material and distributing it, the seepage or percolation through the mass was quickly checked and the barrier became effective.

The struggle was terrific, one of the best in history. After almost two years, the Colorado River was turned back into its channel, where it subsequently found its own way home to the gulf. In June 1907 George Wharton James again circumnavigated the Salton Sea and found the entire volcanic area submerged:

> Not a trace or sign of it remained save the four volcanic buttes, which are now islands . . . I now await with great interest the "going down" of the Salton Sea, and the uncovering of the volcanoes. Will the water have quenched the internal fires? How will the ground be affected? These and other questions I hope to solve soon after the water subsides.

Smeaton Chase also expected the sea to die of evaporation as Ancient Lake Cahuilla had died of evaporation who knows how many times through the proverbial eons of time. "It is at best a rather cheerless object," he wrote in 1919,

> beautiful in a pale, placid way, but the beauty is like that of a mirage, the placidity that of stagnation and death. Charm of color it has, but none of sentiment; mystery, but not romance. Loneliness has its own attraction, and it

is a deep one; but this is not so much loneliness as abandonment, not a solitude sacred but a solitude shunned. Even the gulls that drift and flicker over it seem to have a spectral air, like bird-ghosts banished from the wholesome ocean. But for the Salton the appointed end is but a slow sinking of its bitter, useless waters, a gradual baring of slimy shores, until it comes once more, and probably for the last time, to extinction in dead, hopeless desert.

As to the slow sinking of its waters, the baring of its slimy shore, it never happened. The reason is clear. The sea, having no outlet except evaporation, is being fed by the New and Alamo Rivers faster than it evaporates. The Stinking River, the Foul River would be more fitting names; you could duplicate the color and texture of the water by mixing cans of pea and chicken-noodle soup. These rivers are official dumps where you get rid of things that are dangerous to crops (such as selenium and excess nutrients from fertilizers) or that stink (such as slaughterhouse scraps, raw sewage, and dead farm animals). Their slow currents carry enough detritus of civilization to sicken your average sewer rat and, so I have read, enough infectious agents—hepatitis A, cholera, dysentery, typhoid, polio—to unleash a plague in a city. Watch long enough and all kinds of horrors swirl by en route to the Salton Sea. The drifting, flickering gulls have a good time of it, pecking over the tidbits.

The best of times for the gulls are the worst of times for the talapia, a small grazing fish that was transplanted from Africa to the Imperial Valley (in all likelihood, these fish would have made themselves useful in the weed-choked irrigation ditches had they not found the open waters of the Salton Sea more to their liking). Just what harm the talapia do to the sea is hard to say. What harm the sea does to the talapia is all too easy to see. Virtual tides of dead fish float in the foam at water's edge. Solid layers of dead fish stack on the beaches, exposed to the sun and the well-fed gulls. So powerful is the stench of dead fish, it drifts to Palm Springs fifty miles away, or if the wind is right—or wrong, depending on where you are—it drifts to Arizona, over a hundred miles away.

Besides talapia, the people at the Department of Fish and Game have transplanted other species over the years in an effort to colonize a rather empty Salton Sea. In the 1930s they planted fifteen thousand coho salmon; that is, they introduced a cold-water fish into a warm-water sea. The salmon were never seen again. Neither were the Mexican anchovies they planted, or the halibut or the flounder or the scalyfins or the half a dozen other species they planted. But that's all beside the point because the corvina they planted did survive— thrive is a better word; they grow to the size of tunas. Apparently the talapia die-offs do not affect the corvina. But whether the corvina are safe to eat is questionable. There's no need to post signs. It's only too obvious.

If you care about fishing, the Salton Sea Sickness (to use the worn-out catchphrase) is troubling. The litany of catastrophic bird die-offs makes even sadder reading. In 1992, by conservative estimates, 150,000 eared grebes died from causes unknown (the sick birds staggered ashore and stood still while the gulls began eating them on the spot). In 1994 another 20,000 eared grebes died in the same mysterious fashion. In 1996 more than 20,000 birds died of avian botulism, including over 1,000 endangered brown pelicans (the sick pelicans stumbled ashore, their great, ungainly heads dangling as if their necks had been broken). In 1998 more than 17,000 birds died of avian cholera (and other undetermined diseases), including 6,000 nesting cormorants, the entire population of cormorants on Mullet Island, wiped out at a stroke. As this endless cycle of "wildlife mortality events" continues to puzzle scientists, workers at the wildlife refuge can only continue to collect the casualties for transport to emergency treatment centers, or more often, to the incinerator. It's a grim heart-breaking scene, too easily imagined.

As sea life dwindles, so does sea-going recreation. People no longer come in great numbers like they came in the flush times of the 1940s and 1950s, when this waterfront wonderland saw more visitors than Yosemite. I was among the many who were touched by the place. I close my eyes and I am seven years old again, building castles with my sister on the clean white-sand beaches, the water so warm it gives the air a balmy tropical feel. I am nineteen and on a weekend outing with my party-time college crowd. Our ski boats have been beached. A fire has been lit. Now the wine! And calls to pass around the bota bag. The hours pass. The cumulus clouds stack around the horizon. The sun sets and the moon rises on the moody, ever-changing face of the sea. Never have I seen a body of water so lovely, so overflowing with bird life, deafening and cheering at the same time: the Canada geese in long, disciplined wedges; the cormorants in wavy lines of six, twelve, and twenty; the brown pelicans in polite single file, line after line rising and falling in unison. "I will never forget this," I say to myself.

Every possible solution dreamed up by scientists to save the sea—the Pump-out Option, the Diked Impoundment Option, the Removal of Salt Inflow Option, the Water Import

Option—comes with a price tag in the hundreds of millions. But if the sea is allowed to reach the point where fish can no longer survive, millions of migratory birds will suffer as well, not to mention millions of dollars in real estate within sniffing distance of the stench. Looking beyond the birds, if you restore the sea you will restore sea-going recreation. Picture it: the riverboat casinos, the speed boats in their dozens, rocking gently on their ropes, bumping each other between races, plus sailing, fishing, and golf forever. I trust developers are working on it right now.

* * *

Turning away from the view that has caused this lengthy diversion, I follow the creeks back to camp. This evening, after my unvarying intake of comestibles—except for the serving of sausage, jettisoned into the bushes—I decide to sleep in the open, unencumbered by the tent. I throw my sleeping bag plumb on the pine-needle floor and follow it down. As the evening darkens, the silence becomes more silent, so silent I can hear the dry stalks of corn lilies rustling in Skunk Cabbage Meadow. Encased and cozy between the batting, I open my eyes wide and roam the sky, the clusters of stars hanging close above the black silhouettes of trees. And I think of the sky above Palm Springs, too bright with city lights for celestial moments like this.

The sound of great horned owls fills the night, the deep hooting of the male, the higher hooting of his mate, a haunting harmony. The rise and fall of swallows, viewed through the corn lilies, fills the morning. Like a dream, the rest of the week passes in a series of primitive camps, the fourth day, the fifth, the sixth, all too alike to enumerate, although I note them at tedious length. It was a week well spent and I leave feeling calmer and stronger. As always, I'm sorry when it ends. Later, I say. Later I will come back and spend another week. But *later* is always part of these last moments.

* * *

The last of August settles over the San Jacintos. One by one the days slip by irretrievably, until the best month of the year is over and done. Having spent so much time in the back-country, I want nothing more than to spend September in my shuttered bedroom, flushing out my field notes, setting them straight, separating the worthy from the nonsensical, cutting and pasting them into some kind of order. Now as I add terse marginalia to a series of rough drafts (in October, beside the pool), I realize that if this book is to be published in my life-time I must end it, however painful it is to let go. I have put in my four years of research, during which time I have read nothing and met no one except to further my work. I have visited every place of action, in various ways, at different times. I have followed the old stories wherever they led, tested the stories on my mother, talked them to death, so she no longer listens. (Was this her punishment for taking me in?) The inevitable result is that I think I now know something about our local history. What that means, at its most superfi-cial, is that I can have folksy conversations with the Prickly Pear gang. (Or would they drive me into a corner and take me to task for faulty assumptions and details misconstrued?) I'll leave it to a younger observer with a fresh notebook and a sharp pencil to pick up where my stamina ran out, to carry on with the stories I have started and never finished, to gather in the stray stories and the stories to be.

233

So. Having finished the business of putting everything in order, in what I hope is a worthwhile, meaningful way, having hunted for misspellings and chipped away at verbiage, I snap it up, wrap it up, and send it off. The weeks pass and I find myself putting all my energy not into a new book, but into visualizing the arrival at my mother's doorstep of the tightly-packed carton of books, each volume crisp and trim. A brief period of fuss follows, a flurry of book-signings, the interviews with the stammering author who has no appetite for celebrity.

Ultimately, of course, the silence closes over. Now when an invitation comes my way, I welcome it as a diversion. "Well, what's next?" someone will ask. It's a question for which I have been preparing myself day and night. Although I suppose I could fall into impossible longings, it seems hardly conceivable I shall ever want to leave my private corner of paradise— the cool blue swimming pool, the overfamiliar room with the view, the holidays bewilderingly full of kin. The truth is, I'm at a loss to know how to answer that one. Let's just say I'm between books.